I PLEDGE YOU MY TROTH

I PLEDGE YOU MY TROTH

A Christian View of Marriage,
Family, Friendship

JAMES H. OLTHUIS

1817

Harper & Row, Publishers, San Francisco

New York, Grand Rapids, Philadelphia, St. Louis
London, Singapore, Sydney, Tokyo, Toronto

I PLEDGE YOU MY TROTH. Copyright © 1975 by James H. Olthuis. All rights reserved. Printed in the United States of America. No part of this book may be used or reproduced in any manner whatsoever without written permission except in the case of brief quotations embodied in critical articles and reviews. For information address Harper & Row, Publishers, Inc., 10 East 53rd Street, New York, N.Y. 10022.

FIRST HARPER & ROW PAPERBACK EDITION PUBLISHED IN 1976.

Designed by C. Linda Dingler

Library of Congress Catalog-in-Publication Data

Olthuis, James H.
    I pledge you my throth.

    1. Marriage—Religious aspects—Christianity.
2. Family—Religious life.   3. Friendship—Religious
aspects—Christianity.   I. Title.
BV835.047   1989   248.4   89–15444
ISBN 0-06-066388-X

89   90   91   92   93   MUR   10   9   8   7   6   5   4   3   2   1

CONTENTS

PREFACE

Distressed marriages and fractured families are commonplace. Friendships are few. The search to alleviate hurt and pain has become a cry for help. Why? Why do the relations with the most promise of intimacy so often freeze up and die? Why do they lack zest, vitality, and closeness? Why are they so often bizarre? Why do we so often feel like victims?

Is it time to discard marriage and family and propose entirely new structures? Or do we rehabilitate them? What is the root problem?

This book is one effort to address these life-sized questions—in terms of a biblical framework of reference. I have attempted to avoid simplistic recipes and to investigate rather than merely accept the answers of the past. My concern is to begin—in a fresh manner—to clarify the meaning and purpose of marriage, family, and friendship as God's gifts for the welfare of mankind. In the study I grew in the conviction that the biblical teaching of the copartnership of man and woman under God must be recovered if we are to experience the meaning of liberation, halt our slide into the morass of uncertainty and fear, and regain vibrancy, expectancy, and understanding in marriage, family, and friendship.

It is my hope, intent, and prayer that these pages may be of real benefit and encouragement to all who live in families, enjoy marriages, and long for friendships, to all who seek healing.

This book first began to take shape in the years 1969–71 when I spoke and discussed at various summer conferences sponsored by the Association for the Advancement of Christian Scholarship. Since that time through study and discussion, the material has been extensively reworked and expanded.

I wish to thank Ada Oegema, staff secretary of the Institute for Christian Studies, and Corrie VanderWekken for typing and retyping the manuscript. Willem Hart is to be thanked for the cover illustration which so graphically portrays the meaning of marriage. My special thanks to Bonnie Greene who unstintingly threw herself into the time-consuming task of editing and rewriting. Her dedication has made for a much better, more readable manuscript. I would also like to mention in appreciation my friend and colleague, Arnold De Graaff, with whom many of the ideas in this book were thought through and checked out in hours of pleasant conversation. Finally, I thank Jean, liberated woman and trothful wife, not to forget Douglas and Christine, who add so much sparkle to our lives, for just being who they are.

I Pledge You My Troth is still a sought-after resource in marriage preparation and family seminars, by colleges and universities, especially in Canada and the U.S., in relationships courses, and by persons seeking healing in their relationships. For this reason I have agreed to its re-publication with slight alterations. In the main it is still a fair representation of my present views. However, I do want to call attention to three matters. Although my ideas in 1975 stressed the co-partnership of male and female, my language was regrettably still sexist. In this new edition Harper & Row have agreed to introduce inclusive language in Chapter 1 where it is particularly important. And I ask readers to make the appropriate changes in the remainder of the book. Secondly, I have updated my discussion of "headship" in marriage. Thirdly, where the text reads "Americans," it should read "North Americans."

Since keeping the troth in marriage, family, and friendship is more difficult than pledging troth, I invite readers who find this book helpful to read its sequel, also published by Harper & Row, entitled *Keeping Our Troth: Staying in Love During the Five Stages of Marriage.*

For love, healing, and springtime in our lives and for our planet.

Spring 1989

1

HUMANKIND: MALE AND FEMALE

There is probably no more fascinating index to our society than the classifieds of the *New York Review of Books*. Every month lonely people try to meet each other through ads that describe them as warm, sensuous, brilliant, earthy, cultured, well-traveled, and striking. The people who write these ads aren't salesmen on the road, or housewives isolated in a developing suburb, or even unmarried schoolteachers in rural Vermont. The ads say they live in Manhattan, Toronto, Chicago, Ann Arbor, and Berkeley. The writers claim to be college professors, therapists, artists, business executives, editors, and lawyers. They live in densely populated areas and work in professions that demand daily contact with people. Yet one man's ad sums up the unanimous cry: "Loneliness is awful."

To combat their loneliness, some offer to organize communities of people with common needs and interests—transactional analysis therapy groups, Plato seminars, clubs of unmarried booklovers living in Swarthmore, and even "penfriend" clubs. Others think in smaller terms. They say they want a community of one or maybe two who will share European vacations, sexual fantasies, mushroom-hunting, evenings at the theater, and occasionally marriage.

As sad as these ads are, they are also encouraging because they remind us that the people who read magazines like the *New York Review of Books* are just like everyone else: they want to replace their loneliness with satisfying, close relationships. For years mass circulation magazines have made a good living by advising Americans on their personal relationships. Weight-control specialists have discovered that many obese people can lose enormous amounts of weight on so-called Fat Farms or in small encounter groups where they can develop close relationships with people facing the same problems. And every fund raiser knows that the five-hundred-dollar ticket to a dinner gives supporters a firmer sense of solidarity than a request for a donation at a rally. No matter where people live, no matter what people do, they all need to feel a kinship with other human beings.

Loneliness has plagued people in every society, but probably no group of people has ever had the time or the affluence to worry about their isolation as much as Americans do. If the search for "community" has become a national obsession, it is probably because so many people cannot maintain even the smallest communities—marriage, family, and friendship. Americans may divorce each other at an astonishing rate, but they are just as quick to give marriage another chance. Couples often tell marriage counselors the same tragic story: "Our marriage just didn't work out—we couldn't talk to each other. It's not that we hate each other; we just don't have anything in common anymore." Sometimes one partner or the other will admit that he wouldn't know how to put his marriage back together or to establish a new one because he doesn't even know himself yet.

People who have the insight to recognize such basic problems in their lives are far ahead of others who watch their contrived communities crumbling without really knowing why. Human beings are not neurotic when they long to be close to their husbands or wives, their children, and their friends. Their desires for deep and authentic relationships are part of God's order for his creation.

Whatever form they take in different countries and times, marriage, family, and friendship are also part of God's structural order. If men and women find these relationships unsatisfying and oppressive, something must be wrong with our contemporary ways of establishing marriages, families, and friendships. Abolishing them as archaic institutions and sublimating our needs will not help because we cannot escape God's call to live within the creation order. God has called each of us to live in a faithful relationship with God and with other

2

human beings. Before we can establish the intimate relations with others that God intended, we need to understand what it means to be a human being called into relation with God.

Humankind Is a Unity

Despite the well-documented "battle of the sexes," humankind is a unity. As members of a community given one calling by the Lord, neither man nor woman stands alone. All men and women together form the corporate whole known as humanity. As the creation of God, no single human being can choose whether to be cohuman or inhuman, a companion or a competitor, interdependent or independent. All people exist as fellow creatures who realize themselves in their togetherness and communality. At its roots humanity is cohumanity, that is, we are all associates. To be anything less is to fail to be fully human. As fellow creatures, we realize God's call to partnership by communally fulfilling the covenant mandate: "Fear God, and keep his commandments; for this is the whole . . . of man" (Eccles. 12:13).[1]

The unity of the human calling—to fear God—rests on the unity of the Word of God. At the same time, the human task has many sides, corresponding to the multidimensional character of the Word of the Lord for life ("his commandments"). We cannot adequately define our cohumanity in terms of rationality, morality, animality, or emotionality. Neither can that humanity be defined in terms of itself, in any dimension of itself, or in any combination of dimensions. Our cohumanity can only be defined in terms of service to the Lord.

Faithful or unfaithful, we are servants of the Lord. That is the heart of our very being, the basic meaning of our many-sided existence, the ineradicable structure of our humanity. We are not creatures who also have a calling from the Lord among many other obligations. Our creatureliness is our calling to respond to the Word of God. Any definition of humanity that leaves out God's Word cannot capture our nature as creatures of responsibility.

When Jesus Christ summarized the law as "love God and your

neighbor as yourself," he reaffirmed the Lord's creational intention. From the creation, we have been challenged, invited, and exhorted to show our love for God in concrete acts of service. Since the Fall this service to God, the birthmark as well as the birthright of every person, has been simultaneously a ministry of reconciliation. Although humankind was made in the image of God, all of us now bear the disfiguring marks of the Fall. To regain authentic humanity, we must be remade in the image of the Son of God. Without Christ, humanity, which ought to be service to God and neighbor, is at bottom self-service. True cohumanity is fellow service which is fellowship in Christ.

Humankind Is a Biunity

Even though humankind is one in its calling to serve God, our unity is at the same time a biunity: male and female. Humankind always exists as male and female. Male is no more "human" than woman, and female is no less "human" than male. That is the message of the Scriptures.

"When God created man, he made him in the likeness of God. Male and female he created them, and he blessed them and named them Man when they were created" (Gen. 5:1, 2). Humanity in biunity is male and female. Man and woman are totally different; yet they are both totally human. Jesus reaffirmed God's intention in conversation with the Pharisees: "Have you not read that he who made them from the beginning made them male and female" (Matt. 19:4).

Humankind exists in the female-male duality as a creational given. God did not make two kinds of human beings. Rather, humankind is a twofold being: male and female. Since man and woman belong together, man cannot be defined without woman, nor woman without man.

Nevertheless, in the Lord woman is not independent of man nor man of woman; for as woman was made from man, so man is now born of woman. And all things are from God (1 Cor. 11:11–12).

4

Man and woman function reciprocally and are so delicately related that each feels the effects of the other's failure. Humanity was created male and female, two distinct and correlative creatures, each fully and independently human. At the same time, each is naturally oriented toward the other, existing in a mutual relationship of belonging.

That woman came from man's rib simply and beautifully declares that man and woman together constitute humanity. They came to each other from each other; they belong together. We cannot understand ourselves in relationship to God without expressing simultaneously our relationship to our neighbors, men and women who along with ourselves are *adam* (earth creature).

God did not create woman a "second-class citizen" or an incomplete or imperfect man. The Scriptures emphatically deny this still popular notion, inherited from Aristotle ("we must look upon the female character as being a sort of natural deficiency"), transmitted by Boethius in the Middle Ages ("woman is a temple built upon a sewer"), and more recently given new luster by Freud ("anatomy is destiny").

God created a very good twofold humanity: male and female, open to each other as equal partners. Genesis 2 describes that relationship. Although God stamped all the other works of creation "good" and "very good," God looked at the creation of man and judged it "not good." "It is not good that the man should be alone; I will make him a helper fit for him" (Gen. 2:18). A parade of animals and birds passed by Adam as he searched for a suitable helper. Adam recognized that their natures were different from his own and named them accordingly: tiger, elephant, horse, cattle, eagle, robin, and so on. "But for the man there was not found a helper fit for him" (Gen. 2:20). Then God created woman and brought her to man. Adam's joy was unbounded. Finally he had found a creature like himself. There were certain pleasing differences, but there was also a deep kinship, an unmistakable homogeneity. In her he saw his reflected image. He exclaimed: "This at last is bone of my bones and flesh of my flesh; she shall be called Woman, because she was taken out of Man" (Gen. 2:23).

The Sex Difference Is Good

Man found his partner—woman. Between them sprang up openness, mutuality, reciprocity, and interdependence, as God intended. "And the man and his wife were both naked, and were not ashamed" (Gen. 2:25). The sex difference, which made them male and female, was good from the very beginning. The mutual attraction between the man and the woman came from the Lord; it was not the result of the "doing wrong" or "fall" of the hermaphrodite as Plato imagined in the *Symposium* (189E–191E) and as has been more recently championed by Nicolai Berdyaev.[2]

Christians should take heart at the scriptural account. Many of us are embarrassed at the church's past record on sex. Yet in spite of the world's accusations that the Christian church is afraid of sex and in spite of the fact that the church has often proved itself guilty as charged, the Bible forthrightly states that the male-female sex difference was good from the beginning and that harmonious male-female relations are the creational intention. Properly understood, the biblical view gives a sound basis for full human sexuality. Biblical givens show us the way in today's situation, forcing us to reject any suggestion of male superiority and female inferiority and the corresponding male domination and female subordination as contrary to the partnership proclaimed in Genesis. At the same time, the biblical testimony also contradicts efforts to blur sex differences (a trend that trades on Plato's myth of an original man-woman or hermaphrodite).[3] The Scriptures indicate that male is male and female is female. Together as counterparts they compose humankind.

Man and woman are partners in the richness of their biunity, with the call to be helpmates to each other *everywhere* and in *everything*, not just in marriage and family. The Scriptures are very plain here, embarrassingly so for many.

So God created man in his own image, in the image of God he created him; male and female he created them. And God blessed them, and God said to them, "Be fruitful and multiply, and fill the earth and subdue it; and have dominion over the fish of the sea and over the birds of the air and over every living thing that moves upon the earth (Gen. 1:27–28).

Regrettably, male prejudice has encouraged many to suggest that only part of this mandate refers to woman. Her role is to be fruitful, to multiply, and to fill the earth, but that is as far as she may go. The other parts of the mandate—conquering the earth and mastering its creatures—are male prerogatives. Despite its longevity, this tradition finds no grounds in the Scriptures.

Human Sexuality Is Total

When we say that God created human beings, male and female, we are affirming that we are through and through sexual beings. Human sexuality is a total thing, not simply one-dimensional. Maleness and femaleness affect everything we do. Human sexuality must not be reduced to a physical, biotic, or even psychic difference because it has as many expressions as there are aspects to human existence.

If, for instance, human sexuality were merely physical functioning, why should we shrink from changing partners at random just as machines are replaced when there is a breakdown or when a new model appears? However, reducing human sexuality to the physical dehumanizes us and prevents the growth of human relationships. We become machines, or at best animals.

Sexuality affects everything human, not just marriage. A woman walks, talks, thinks, feels, loves, believes, writes, paints, and buys as a woman. A man walks, talks, thinks, feels, loves, believes, writes, paints, and buys as a man. Both ways are human ways. To despise either way is to despise the creation. Male and female sexuality decisively influences all human relationships, most obviously marriage and the family but all others as well.

This is not an endorsement of such traditional sex stereotypes as "men are logical and women are illogical." Henry Higgins reflected

7

our peculiar belief in the inferior intellect of women when he sang his misguided lament in *My Fair Lady.* *

> Why can't a woman be more like a man?
> Women are irrational
> Their heads are full of cotton, hay and rags. . . .
> Why can't a woman learn to use her head?
> Why is thinking something women never do?
> Why is logic never even tried?
> Straightening up their hair is all they ever do.
> Why don't they straighten up the mess that's inside?

Similarly, the typical stereotypes for a "real man" (independent, self-reliant, achievement oriented, aggressive) and a "real woman" (dependent, compliant, nurturant, gentle) are misleading popular myths reinforced by false psychological theories rather than outlines describing the created nature of men and women. When such stereotypes become standards for the "normal" man or woman, they are dangerous, especially for those who are developing into manhood and womanhood. Must a man question his virility if he acts gently and compassionately? Is a woman a traitor to the female species if she is achievement oriented, enjoys competition, and is aggressive? Should a young man doubt his masculinity if he does not idolize physical strength and prefers teaching kindergarten? Should a young woman fear losing her femininity if she discovers she has a mechanical bent?

In every instance the answer is beyond debate; yet these prevalent stereotypes lead us to doubt our masculinity or femininity in such situations until we find ourselves in an identity crisis. We feel anxious, guilty, effeminate, or emasculated. No matter how many men and women may fit the traditional stereotypes, it is preposterous and fatuous to conclude that these characteristics belong to the very structural makeup of male and female. The only justifiable conclusion is that we are the way we are because of nurture. Surely it is hypocritical—

*Book and lyrics by Alan Jay Lerner, music by Frederick Loewe, adapted from George Bernard Shaw's play and Gabrial Pascal's motion picture, *Pygmalion*.

even blasphemous—to plead "created nature" and blame God for the painful distortion we have brought into male-female relationships.

Partnership Becomes Subordination

The extent of our distortion becomes clear when we return to the Genesis account. After the good beginning recorded in Genesis 2, humankind broke with the Lord. Genesis 3 records how man and woman chose to believe in the word of the serpent and refused to live by the Word of God. This was the Fall: by which death, distortion, and the lie entered creation. The break with God brought an immediate break in our relations with ourselves, our neighbors, and the rest of creation. When man's heartfelt communion with God and his neighbor broke, he set himself over against woman; woman, likewise, reacted against man.

The man and the woman felt the Fall's effect immediately. "Then the eyes of both were opened, and they knew that they were naked" (Gen. 3:7). With the Fall, intimacy became a curse instead of a blessing, openness meant vulnerability, dependence felt like defenselessness, and mutuality turned into hostility. Fearing the exposure of their hearts' intent, man and woman covered up in order to keep a safe distance from each other, and together they tried to hide from God.

They discovered, though, that nothing can hide or be hidden from the eyes of the Lord. When God confronted him with his faithlessness, man dropped his pretensions and turned on his companion. "It was the woman you put with me" (Gen. 3:12, JB). The woman protested and shifted the blame to the serpent. In effect, both pointed the finger of accusation at God the creator of all. Their search for a scapegoat for their sins became a pattern that has remained with us since the Fall. Neither man nor woman is willing to bear the responsibility for sin.

Sin distorted the relation between man and woman from a helping-and-needing-each-other biunity to a denying-and-hindering-each-other disunity. No longer a helpmate, woman would become a competitor rather than a companion. Man would take advantage of the woman's natural yearning for him in order to rule over her. In pain she would give birth to children (Gen. 3:16). That was the curse the Lord pronounced upon the man and woman, and through them on the entire creation.

Thus, what has been called the battle of the sexes is actually the abnormal result of the Fall. Man-in-sin will attempt to dominate woman as if she were just a part of the creation to be put under his feet; yet man himself is also cursed and the entire creation with him. Because of sin, man's dominion over the earth will be nothing but toil and trouble, blood, sweat, and tears. Even though the wages of sin are depicted in the specific human tasks of breadwinning and child-bearing, the intention is clearly universal. Whatever men and women do, their lives will reap trouble and sorrow.

Two other matters require brief comment. First the curse fell on the man and the woman equally, a fact we often forget. In "sorrow" woman would bring forth children, and in "sorrow" man would get his bread from the ground. (Gen. 3:16–17).[4] Second, our predominantly physical readings of the terms *naked, ashamed, desire,* and *sorrow* run counter to the whole thrust of the passages. Ignoring these two points can lead to such chauvinistic tactics as declaring anesthetic in childbirth unbiblical while relieving farming "sorrow" is perfectly legitimate, even if that involves today's air-conditioned tractor cabs.

It is important to emphasize that the curses of the Lord are just that—curses, not commands to be obeyed. They are the Lord's infallible descriptions of humankind's future in sin. The domination of man and the subordination of woman is a distortion of the original intention of the creator. When we ignore God's order, we plunge ourselves into disorder. Disobedience pulls down the curse of God's Word upon the people and the creation. When God told man and woman that their sin would bring judgment to the creation instead of blessing, the words of the curse demonstrated that Jehovah God maintains the original Word to us, whether for life or for death.

Thus, the words of curse are not norms to guide our male-female relations. For instance, the curse does not mean that man ought to rule over woman or that man and woman ought to live in pain. The disorder of the Fall is not to become the order we try to maintain. Too often Christians defend injustice and distorted relations on the grounds that the "order of the Fall" (which I can only call *dis*order) cancels out the order for creation.[5]

The Truth Versus the Lie

With sin, the antithesis became a reality in the world. The Thesis of the Lord, the Word, is forever opposed by the Antithesis, the Lie of the Devil. Since the Fall the Spirit of Obedience and the Spirit of Disobedience have been working at cross-purposes in creation. No one and nothing remain unaffected by it. If our eyes have been opened in Christ, we will see the sin of our own hearts and the real nature of the antithesis as the battle of competing spirits; if not, we will attempt to localize sin in a scapegoat, particularly in something exclusively creaturely. Once we place sin outside of ourselves and handle it, we feel free to excuse ourselves from all guilt.

The Genesis account recorded our first attempts to find a scapegoat. Adam accused Eve; Eve accused the serpent. Since then humankind has picked up relative differences in creation and treated them as if they were the antithesis between good and evil. Once we saw the antithesis between black and white. Today we more commonly speak of the distinction between rich and poor as if it were the antithesis between good and evil. Some distinctions pass out of fashion, but the antithesis between man and woman has continued indefatigably down to our own day. Man is pitted against woman; yet he is also bound to her and cannot live without her. Woman finds herself in the same predicament.

Anthropologists have pointed out the effects of this antithesis in tribal cultures where man is sometimes thought to have godlike dominion over woman. In other cultures woman is thought to have superior, if make believe, powers over the man. Sometimes man is evil and woman is good; other times woman is evil and man is good. As Margaret Mead has pointed out:

In every known society, mankind has elaborated the biological division of labor into forms often very remotely related to the original biological differences that provided the original clues. Upon the contrast in bodily form and function, men have built analogies between sun and moon, night and day, goodness and evil, strength and tenderness, steadfastness and fickleness, endurance and vulnerability. Sometimes one quality has been assigned to one sex, sometimes to the other.[6]

The Feminine Mystique

Although a few cultures have considered women the central figures, most have assigned them an inferior role. This has gone on for so long that women have actually believed in their inferiority, a development that Betty Friedan called the "feminine mystique."[7] Historically, this subordination of the female has been tied to male jealousy and fear.

Male jealously of woman is expressed, for example, in the rituals and initiation ceremonies of most primitive tribes. In certain cultures, in a practice called couvade, the father takes to his bed and groans as if in pain when the mother delivers a baby. Although the mother soon returns to work, the father remains in bed for days, showered with attention from friends and relatives. Among the Arapesh of New Guinea a father must lie down with the mother and child immediately after birth so that the child can receive its life-soul from the father or the mother. The father is said to be "in bed having a baby."

Envious of woman's ability to rid herself of evil humors through menstruation, tribesmen of central Australia, among others, practiced subincision (slitting of the penis the length of the urethra) on adolescent boys so that they could be like women. Periodically the wound was reopened so the males could simulate menstruation. Other tribes operated on girls at puberty in a rite called infibulation. Early Roman customs of dealing with newborn children illustrate this pervasive male envy of the female. Among the Romans the child was allowed to live only if the father raised it from the ground, an act which signified the real formal birth of the child. At that moment the child was initiated into the household religion. This Roman custom was the source of our phrase "to raise a child."[8]

In their ignorance of conception, men in some cultures became jealous of women because they alone could bear children. Therefore, man asserted his superiority over woman by transforming his penis from the instrument of the womb to the rod of male power. At the same time, woman's role as childbearer had to be belittled until woman became *only* a womb or an incubator. Man came to see himself as the real bearer of the seed of life which he planted in the female womb. Clearly, the woman's function was secondary. Life was passed on by the father through the mother's womb. For instance, Aeschylus (525–456 B.C.) has Apollo say in *Eumenides:*

Not the true parent is the woman's womb that bears the child; she doth but nurse the seed new-sown: the male is the parent; she for him as stranger for a stranger, hoards the germ of life.[9]

Early philosophers and scientists joined in the effort to downgrade the function of the woman. Woman was called flesh, the material mobilized to life by the male Vital Spark or First Cause. The male semen was the spiritual seed, the real giver of life; the female merely supplied the raw material and nourishment for that life. Not until the nineteenth century did Mendel's experiments reveal the equal contribution of the sexes to the heredity of the child.

Even then man clung to the illusion that he alone was lord of creation. Although woman was just as essential in conception, man kept her in subjugation even as he idealized and glorified her. She was needed at home where her femaleness could be fulfilled in her task as mother, laundress, maid, nurse, governess, cook, and wife. The family was often misused as an institution to keep the female in her place. Women stayed home, had babies, and looked after the man of the house.

As the necessity for woman to stay at home decreased, man played up her frail beauty and utter helplessness—with emphasis on the "frail" and "utter." Man carefully sheltered woman in an ill-concealed effort to protect his own rights. By and large the majority of women did not rebel. Dependency and subordination brought just enough benefits that many women didn't mind the roles men prescribed for them. Even today male-female relations remain much the same. Women are still reduced to womb and breasts, preferably well developed and displayed. They learn early that pleasing men pays off. As some women themselves are saying: "All women are hookers, but some are a little bit more honest about it."

Against this background it is most understandable that men are deeply threatened by women's liberation. If women actually stopped falling for the male line and became persons in their own right, they would have to be dealt with as equals with rights. Once again we are at the crux of the problem. Since the Fall, man has been desperately afraid of recognizing that a woman is his equal, his helpmate, his companion. Therefore, he has consistently tried to reduce her to something less than himself, a being he both loves and detests. Woman was either raised to the level of hallowed saint and praised as the all-good, tender, passionless Madonna of heaven, or she was lowered to the level of the vulgar sinner and berated as the all-evil, seductive, lascivious witch of Satan. Either she was an object of adoration or a vessel of lust; a virgin or a harlot. In neither case was she allowed to be what God wanted her to be: woman.

Why not? Because man desired all the glory for himself and was afraid that the woman would get the upper hand and knock him from his self-styled pedestal. Indeed, this is exactly what some feminists have in mind. Although they have seen much of the problem clearly, their efforts to achieve a power takeover offer no real promise for the future. To attempt to dominate men is only to perpetuate the disorder of the Fall. Both man and woman must climb down from their pedestals and learn to rule creation together as servants under God.

The Church and the Female Put-down

Though tribal peoples and society as a whole have clearly raised a false antithesis between man and woman, the record of the Christian church is equally bad and certainly less excusable. The church fathers in general wrote as if women were temptresses to be shunned. Tertullian called women the "gate of hell."[10] Augustine speculated that "the woman together with her own husband is the image of God . . . the woman herself alone, then she is not the image of God; but as regards the man alone, he is the image of God."[11] Yet, beginning in the fourth century theologians also began to talk about Mary Mother of God. Slowly, Holy Mary was placed over against profane Eve.

The views of the church fathers are well documented in recent literature on the "woman question."[12] Of more concern to modern readers is the church's unwillingness to shake off the archaic and mistaken notion of the inferiority and subordination of women. Because the church has read the Western put-down of woman into Scripture, the church has affirmed the status quo when it really needed to be reformed. I do not believe it is any exaggeration to say that even today women generally suffer from a sugar-coated put-down.[13] Despite all the nice words and protestations to the contrary, the church and the larger society have not yet recognized the female as an equal partner alongside the male. Nor does the church or society recognize that male and female *together* constitute "man," that neither partner is superior to the other, and that both are united in service to God.

The female put-down is not only pervasive and tenacious, but it is also so thoroughly unbiblical that this first chapter was essential. If we are to recover biblical views of marriage, family, and friendship, we must accept the full personhood of both male and female. The Bible simply does not put down woman as woman. It puts down sin in male as well as in female. Human sin is responsible for disorder, including the subordination of woman. God had (and in Jesus Christ *has*) other

15

intentions: a new creation with male-female partnership in God's name and to God's glory.

NOTES

1. The last phrase of this verse is most often translated "the whole duty of man." However, the word *duty* is not in the Hebrew text. I have deleted it because it obscures the biblical teaching that obedience to God's commands is not simply a duty which we have but the mark and definition of our very existence as human.

2. See Nicolai Berdyaev, *Destiny of Man* (New York: Harper and Row, 1966).

3. Although Simone de Beauvoir in *The Second Sex* (New York: Alfred A. Knopf, 1957) does not endorse the androgyne myth as such, sexuality (femininity and masculinity) must be transcended in order to be free and autonomous.

4. Unfortunately many translations obscure the equality under the curse by employing different words to translate the same Hebrew word. Happily the parallel is clear in the KJV.

5. See the Appendix, "Paul on Women," for further discussion of how this confusion has undone our exegesis of the New Testament passages on women.

6. Margaret Mead, *Male and Female* (New York: Morrow, 1949) p. 7.

7. Betty Friedan, *The Feminine Mystique* (New York: Norton, 1963). For an introduction to modern feminism, see Robin Morgan, ed., *Sisterhood Is Powerful* (New York: Random House, 1970) and Vivian Gornick and Barbara K. Moran, eds., *Women in Sexist Society* (New York: Basic Books, 1971).

8. The anthropological material describing these practices is immense and constantly growing. For an introduction to some of the material, see Norman Bell and Ezra Vogel, eds., *A Modern Introduction to the Family* (New York: Free Press, 1968); David and Vera Mace, *Marriage—East and West* (New York: Doubleday, 1960); Margaret Mead, *Male and Female*; Ashley Montagu, *The Natural Superiority of Women* (New York: Macmillan, 1954); Richard Lewinsohn, *A History of Sexual Customs* (New York: Harper and Row, 1958).

9. Aeschylus, *The Eumenides, The Complete Greek Drama*, vol. 1, ed. Whitney Oates and Eugene O'Neill (London: Random House), p. 294.

10. Tertullian, *On the Apparel of Women*, I, i *The Ante-Nicene Fathers*, vol. 4 (Grand Rapids: Eerdmans, 1965), p. 14.

11. Augustine, *On the Trinity* VII, 10; *The Nicene and Post-Nicene Fathers*, vol. 3 (Grand Rapids: Eerdmans, 1956), p. 159.

12. For a detailed study of the early christian church's view of marriage, John T. Noonan's *Contraception* (New York: Mentor, 1965) is extremely valuable. Roland H. Bainton's *Sex, Love, and Marriage* (London: Fontana Books, 1958) is a simple, readable Christian survey of the material. Morton M. Hunt's *The Natural History of Love* (New York: Alfred Knopf, 1959) is a well-written history of sex and marriage in the Western world. Derrick S. Bailey's *Sexual Relations in Christian Thought* (New York: Harper and Row, 1959) and Vern L. Bullough's *The Subordinate Sex* (Chicago: University of Illinois Press, 1973) are helpful volumes.

13. Larry Christenson's *The Christian Family* (Minneapolis: Bethany Fellowship, 1970) and Marabel Morgan's *The Total Woman* (Old Tappan, New Jersey: Fleming H. Revell Company, 1973) are two popular examples of such sugar-coated put-down within the Christian community. Christenson's commendable call to "God's order" for marriage and family is seriously marred by his mistaken assumption that a woman can only indirectly—through man—relate to God and the rest of society. This enables him to preach subordination and submission, not as a harsh male imposition, but a God-given "means of protection," "social balance," and "spiritual power" which women should freely choose because it is for their own good (chap. 2). "God's intention is that a husband should stand between his wife and the world, absorbing many of the physical, emotional and spiritual pressures which would come against her. It is the husband, not the wife, who is primarily responsible for what goes on in the home, the community and the church" (p. 37). After all, "the heart of a woman is more easily discouraged and dejected. God has made her that way" (p. 128).

Marabel Morgan's advice to wives seeking happiness in marriage is an unadulterated plea for the playboy-playgirl, he-man, sex-bomb mentality—unbelievably—baptized with a Christian veneer. "Let him know he's your hero" (p. 60). Let him be "free to do what he wants" (p. 52). "Treat him like a king and cater to his needs" (p. 68). Graciously adapt to his way, even if you know it's wrong (p. 71). If you do, "he may even choose to do exactly what you've been wanting!" (p. 56). If you don't fulfill his needs, especially sexually, he'll look elsewhere. "If you are stingy in bed, he'll be stingy with you" (p. 112). Tell him you crave his body (p. 127). "Never let him know what to expect when he opens the front door; make it like opening a surprise package. You may be a smoldering sexpot, or an all-American fresh beauty. Be a pixie, or a pirate—a cow-girl or a show girl. Keep him off guard" (p. 95). It is especially distressing that this is reputed to be a Christian way. The underlying idea that wives can count on the infidelity of their husbands—which leads to a frantic effort to keep him interested—runs directly counter to the biblical idea of marriage which stresses the mutual commitment of troth allowing each partner to count on each other's fidelity.

On the other hand, thankfully a book was recently published (when this work was at press) which does much to demonstrate the unbiblical character of the female put-down. In fact, *All We're Meant To Be* by Letha Scanzoni and Nancy Hardesty (Waco, Texas: Word Books, 1974) in many ways complements this present volume.

MARRIAGE: TROTH, ROMANCE, AND SEX

Marriage is under attack today. In itself that is nothing new. Marriage has always had its share of discreditors, but seldom have so many people openly questioned the value of marriage. Although most people still marry, many think of an affair as not only inevitable but highly desirable as an antidote to the boredom of a long marriage. The crisis of our society is reflected in the hypocrisy of people who pay lip service to marriage while they live in broken marriages or nonchalantly have an affair. Many talk the old morality and live the new. Nevertheless there is real hope for change.

Marriage Is a Unique Calling

Man and woman are to be helpmates to each other in all the different callings of their lives. In obedience to God, men and women will love each other as fellows in Jesus Christ. We are all neighbors, but we are also individuals with the callings, talents, and characters we need to do our own task and to fulfill humanity's calling. Though we're all part of the human community, we can't be partners with everyone in all the different tasks facing us. Not every neighbor makes a suitable co-worker in education, politics, art, commerce, recreation, or whatever. One person lacks insight; we can't develop congenial relations with another; and the third lives too far away. What's true for work communities is doubly true for marriage—not every neighbor is suitable to be one's helpmate.

"Well, that's obvious," we say. Yet quite a few Americans are living as if it weren't so obvious, as if one neighbor makes as good a marriage partner as another. Some claim we marry the first person who comes along when we decide we simply can't stay single any longer. Others claim that living in a group where everyone is "married" is the only way to maintain humane and nonelitist relationships. Divorce statistics also suggest that quite a few people marry without knowing what kind of neighbor would make a good marriage partner. If many of us marry because it "feels right," we may be part of a vast crowd that can't do anything else because no one has a very clear idea of what marriage is.

Marriage Is Troth

God gave his Word for marriage when he said, "Therefore a man leaves his father and his mother and cleaves to his wife, and they become one flesh" (Gen. 2:24). And Christ added: "They are no longer two, therefore, but one body. So then, what God has united, man must not divide" (Matt. 19:6, JB).

God called husband and wife to an exclusive, lifelong partnership of love, or as I prefer, a partnership of troth or fidelity. In a sentence, marriage is a mutual, permanent, exclusive, one-flesh union between husband and wife, characterized by troth or fidelity.

Physical intercourse is an important part of being "one flesh," but the key concept in marriage is troth. If a married couple obeys the central love-command, they will be faithful to each other. Troth involves loyalty, trust, love, devotion, reliability: a husband can count on his wife, and she on him. Troth is not an act which occurs now and then; rather marriage is a state or institution in which troth ought to characterize all its many aspects. Physical intercourse grows out of this troth-intercourse and consummates it as a good gift of the Lord in marriage. Without masks or pretenses, husband and wife grow together and strengthen the bond of love between them.

Mutual dependence and trust allow husband and wife to be genuine and real with each other. Each can be accepted and loved for what he is. A wife need not compete with other women for her husband's love and affection; she has it. Her husband has sworn a bond of lifelong troth to her to which God is the witness. Neither does the husband have to compete with other men for his wife's continued attention. Both of them settled that matter when they married. That is the very meaning of marriage: both partners count on the other's fidelity. This is crucially important because it is contrary to much current theory and practice in North America, where husbands and wives usually live under the constant fear of losing each other. The effect of such tension on their marriages is disastrous.

Men and women who marry in Christ share a mutual trust. They can be sure of their relationship because it rests on God's covenantal faithfulness. They also know that through his Word for marriage, God brought them together and keeps them together.

Troth

Marriage is a partnership of troth. Likewise, troth is the key to intimacy in family and friendship. Yet, in spite of its importance, few people are consciously aware of troth. Even the term is unfamiliar. Since the very heart of this book is a plea for the recovery of troth (it could well be entitled the "troth book"), we need to interrupt our discussion of marriage to consider the meaning of troth more carefully.

Troth is an Old English term for truth, faithfulness, loyalty, and honesty. The single word *troth* captures the nuances of trust, reliability, stability, scrupulousness, ingenuousness, authenticity, integrity, and fidelity. To be fickle, capricious, unreliable, shifty, whimsical, disloyal, rootless, perfidious is to be anything but trothful.

The call to troth is a unique dimension of the call to be human, the call to love God and our neighbor. God's call to love is many-sided: we are to be truthful, just, and thrifty in all our doings; we are to execute our responsibilities with style, taste, dignity, and conviction; we are to take care of ourselves and the rest of creation with sensitivity and

21

concern. God's call to be human also means we must answer the invitation to troth. By nature, man responds to this call; he cannot escape it. In part, humanity means pledging troth or breaking troth, counting on others or distrusting them, keeping one's word or playing fast and loose with one's promises, being authentic or being hypocritical.

If men and women respond positively to the troth call, their lives acquire new depth and meaning. People can count on each other, and counting on one another leads to understanding and sharing, to integrity, genuineness, and commitment. Troth is the staying power which gives special joy and color to intimacy in family, friendship, and marriage. Troth is the moral expression of love just as justice is its jural expression and thrift its economic expression. Troth, justice, thrift, truth, style, dignity, and certainty are all sides of life. When these dimensions of life are developed out of a heart commitment to Jesus Christ, they become the fruits of faith, the responses of love. If our keeping troth is grounded in our commitment to Jesus Christ—what the Scriptures call faith, hope, and love—then it becomes an integral part of the covenantal faithfulness between God and man.

Marriage Is of the Lord for Men and Women

Modern sociologists, such as Lionel Tiger and Robin Fox,[1] ignore God's call to troth in marriage and insist that marriage is merely a human invention to be eliminated whenever we please. Lately they have pointed out that marriage is not found among chimpanzees as evidence that it is our own invention. However, instead of undermining marriage as they believe, this argument actually strengthens the biblical view of marriage as a human arrangement not found among animals. Animals mate according to instinctual patterns, but men and women have to choose with whom they will live. Furthermore, they have to choose to stick together no matter what happens. Men and women have to work at their marriages, and that leaves them room to mess things up. This does not mean, however, that marriage is an invention of man. Rather, marriages occur between men and women only because God made marriages possible by issuing his Word for marriage. Human marriages exist as an unfolding of this Word for marriage. Mankind cannot do away with marriage simply because God's words never fail; one of those unfailing words is the Word for marriage.

Since marriage is of the Lord, husband and wife live together under the Word of God for marriage. In the beginning God's Word called marriage into being. Now the Scriptures republish that Word for our benefit. Marriage is not just a human invention or merely a social convention. It is the Lord's institution for men and women.

Monogamy Is the Norm

Since the creation, mankind has responded in many different ways to God's Word for marriage. Although the various forms of marriage are all responses to the one norm, some forms reflect more clearly the biblical norm and some less clearly. Since Scripture teaches that marriage is between one husband and one wife, monogamy is the form of marriage which meets the biblical norm.

On the other hand, polygamy goes against the norm of monogamy for marriage. Polygamy is not simply a husband having many wives, but a husband involved in many marriages. The troth fellowship of marriage cannot be shared with more than one husband or wife in the full way that marriage demands. The shared ecstasy, mutual intimacy, open communication, fellow-feeling, and the common struggles which make up a total marriage are difficult enough for a husband and wife to work out together; they are impossible with more than one husband and wife. The fact that face-to-face intimacy in physical intercourse is only possible between two people at the same time is typical of the relationship as a whole. Interestingly enough, plural marriages such as polygamy (many wives) and polyandry (many husbands) always appear to involve individual legal contracts between one man and each of his wives or one wife and each of her husbands.

23

In advocating monogamy as the norm, I am not saying that it is merely the best way to regulate our sexual activities; neither am I saying that men are polygamous by nature. From there it would be but a short step to conclude that fidelity is as unnatural a state as most postwar sociologists claim. From there, of course, it would be an even shorter step to conclude that marriage is no longer necessary and is on the way out in our enlightened age. With all this I vigorously disagree.

Monogamy—not polygamy—is "natural" for man because only monogamy fosters authenticity, sharing, and helping—the cardinal signs of genuine humanity. Of course, man does have a hard time opening himself up and putting aside his deep desires to serve himself, and in the process, he mistrusts others and pulls them down with him. Still, man benefits from opening himself up, despite the dangers. Man and woman have the deep and uniquely human need and responsibility to engage in relationships which deepen, strengthen, and reveal what it means to be man instead of an animal or a tree or a stone. The Lord gave man marriage to help him experience such meaning in life. The marriage bond of troth has the unique character of being so intense that only two people can share in it to the full.

Most modern sociologists commit the same crime against men and women together that Freud committed against women when he declared that "anatomy is destiny." In fact, they begin at the wrong place when they declare monogamy unnatural and polygamy natural just because men and women can have physical intercourse at random, just because a woman has an apparently limitless capacity for orgasm, and so on. Ironically, many feminists (rightly) dispute Freud's apothegm and then turn right around (wrongly, I believe) and discredit monogamous marriage on the basis of their anatomy.

Both the feminists and the sociologists go wrong because they allow the physical, biotic, and psychic to become the most important levels of human existence. The physical element dominates in things, the biotic in plants, and the psychic in animals, but in man the physical, biotic, and psychic dimensions await further unfolding and development. Since they do provide the foundation for total life, we cannot ignore these dimensions. But to consider them overriding determinations for human life is simply to become a slave of one's passions and drives.

When we call man a polygamous creature, we still reduce men and women to sexual objects. Polygyny deprives a woman of her equality, as polyandry deprives men. Although monogamy has often been used by men to keep women in their place (preferably supine), it is the only form of marriage that has the potential to allow a man and woman to live up to the deeply satisfying relationship that marriage is meant to be. Although monogamy itself deserves criticism for the distortions that have occurred within it, it is regressive to turn to polygamy or to reject marriage altogether.

Contrary to popular myth, marriage is not basically a social arrangement to regulate physical intercourse. At heart it is an ethical relationship of troth, affecting the humanity of man at one of its deepest levels. Man is responsible to choose a partner in marriage. This partner is his full partner in troth, not simply his bed partner. From time to time physical intercourse becomes a unique sign of the intense and exclusive relationship between them, as well as a way of reinforcing and strengthening the troth. In the long run physical intercourse is only satisfying and meaningful to human beings when enjoyed in the context of mutual commitment and troth. Ironic as some may find it, the physical in man only gets its due, only develops and opens up fully when it is not the primary focus.

Troth Is Not Arbitrary

Since marriage is of the Lord, each individual marriage takes its life from the Word of God which called marriage into existence. Marital troth, then, does not depend on the arbitrary whims of the man and woman. Marriage is intended to be a permanent trust for life.

The norm of troth (the Word of God for marriage) is quite different

25

from the actual troth or lack of it in individual marriages. A man and a woman who make a commitment of troth to each other are responding to the Lord's norm. Throughout their relationship life is good, happy, and blessed if it continues to move in the way the Lord desires, that is, on the track of troth. The norm inviting troth offers the freedom to respond in so many ways that a pledge of troth or fidelity does not make marriage a life-sentence to boredom but a chance for deep sharing and intimacy. The duty of troth or fidelity is not a burden to restrict or limit man's craving to fulfill his "animal" appetites. The norm of troth is not an ideal superimposed on the physical realities. Nor is it a big stick with which partners can shame each other into submission (often calling God in as witness) or expose their failures. Troth in marriage means that the marriage is a marriage—period. Marital troth is dependent on the norm of troth. And insofar as a man and a woman strive to meet that norm in their relationship, they will find that their commitment is not a burden or a restriction, but an opportunity for even richer experiences, a support to fall back on in hard times, and an invitation to intimacy. The norm becomes a reality in their life together, one they can appeal to, struggle with, and delight in.

When a man and a woman mutually assent to the norm of troth, they begin to experience the blessing and exhilaration it brings. The norm of troth becomes a daily guideline to help them develop their unique life pattern within the basic troth framework. Their goal is a style of living that maximizes troth and thus produces the greatest satisfaction for both of them.

In good times the norm of troth becomes a joyful reality that daily takes a couple along and leads them into new and richer experiences; in difficult times troth is a ready support that holds the couple together even as it pushes them along. In times of conflict the norm quietly but persistently reminds the couple that the issue must be resolved or it will gradually undermine the entire relationship; in times of betrayal the norm of troth is the unwelcome but firm presence that urges the unfaithful partner to a change of heart as it rebukes the couple and visits them with the dire results.

Headship in Marriage

Headship in marriage is central to the discussion of troth; yet most moderns think it is old-fashioned and not even worth debating. For the rest, headship means that the husband is number one and the issue is not debatable. Both positions—with all their refinements—miss the point. Headship has to do in the first place with the main direction of the marriage. Headship points to the important reality that a marriage divided against itself cannot stand. Both partners must be committed to moving in one direction, and united in answering the central questions: What is the meaning of marriage? What are its overriding goals? What vision is going to guide day-to-day activities and decisions? If a husband and wife cannot agree on these questions, their marriage will not grow and deepen but will always be unsettled and in some kind of upheaval. Likewise, a common life-vision is a very important issue a man and woman must consider in choosing a marriage partner.

In marriage headship has to do with the mutual empowerment of equals to be one in troth. Wives as well as husbands share this office. In biblical times, due to the inferior position of women in respect to men, the headship of husbands was emphasized (cf. Appendix, p. 137ff. on meaning of "head"). Husbands were not to hold down or put down their wives. Rather husbands were called to honor, respect, protect, empower, and lift up their wives as equals, as Christ gave himself for the Church. Today, as we are gradually coming to accept the complete equality of men and women, both wives and husbands are called to honor, respect, protect, and if need be, lift up their partners as equals. When both husband and wife exercise their office in love and mutuality, both will be freed to be themselves and their troth will deepen. Clearly, headship has nothing to do with being boss.

Neither does headship imply inferiority or superiority. Rather, headship is a special office of service so that the marriage may thrive and grow. Once a man and woman have decided which vision of life is going to norm their activities in the marriage, they can leave the decisions in day-to-day affairs to the partner with the appropriate talents, temperaments, and situations. Both husband and wife need to be on guard continually so that the "little" things do not develop into the kinds of patterns that undermine the entire marriage.

This interpretation of headship is not common because most interpreters have confused the order for creation and the disorder of the Fall.[2] The result has often been a myopic focus on the ruling of the husband rather than on partnership. Therefore, they had difficulty interpreting headship in terms of the mutual empowerment of equals and tended to treat the husband himself as norm.

Even the much-maligned Paul emphasizes the mutuality of the troth between a husband and wife (cf. Appendix, p. 144). Paul does not say that wives have to be subject to their husbands—period. They are to be subject "as is fitting in the Lord" (Col. 3:18). The wife's subjection is to the Word of God for marriage; that means being a wife and helping the husband so that the two of them can keep the norm for marriage, the word of troth. That is Paul's concern, one that we often overlook in our zeal to put the husband in a superior position. Only when both husband and wife act as servants, loving and submitting to one another, are marriages pleasing to the Lord. We are subject to the Lord by means of the office God has called us to, whether it be husband or wife. We need to remember that these offices are in marriage and are therefore under the law of troth. Neither the husband nor the wife can demand anything of his/her partner that is inconsistent with that troth. Neither the husband may lord it over his wife (a perpetual danger), nor the wife over her husband (an imminent danger in Paul's day and often in ours.)

Marriage Is a Human Task

The Lord gave man marriage so that husbands and wives could enjoy growing strong together. Since marriage is a *human* community, the troth relationship in marriage is not an automatic gift; instead, it must be worked at. Husband and wife must "make love," that is, they need to work out their love on the physical level, but also on every other level of their life together. Husband and wife need to grow together in troth in many ways—in worship, in socializing, in discussions, in life-styles, in likes and dislikes. They need to explore the meaning of justice together, to share the delights of a play or a piece of music, to shop together. But it all takes effort, while physical intercourse comes rather easily to most people. (Although even sex is becoming a problem because of the over-emphasis our society gives it. If we would believe the popular press, impotence and lack of orgasm are the number one problems in America!) What does come hard to those of us raised in this society is troth. Our children do not need physical sex education; they need troth education. Only in the context of marital troth does attention to the mechanics, techniques, and feelings of physical intercourse really have meaning.

Troth Is Not Physical Sex

We often loosely use the word *love* for the troth of fidelity of marriage; yet troth is neither physical sex nor romantic feeling. Intercourse is important, of course, as the culmination and seal of marital troth. Even the law recognizes that a marriage without intercourse is not consummated. However, intercourse must be guided by troth. A man or woman only surrenders his body to another person when both of them have committed themselves to each other. If troth were simply physical sex, human intercourse would be only animal copulation.

If love were just sex, the racing of blood, the rushing of hormones, couples could make sure they were in love with a quick physiological test, like the breath-alyzer—above .8 percent would mean they were in love; below .8 percent, they were not. But that is ridiculous. A person in love is not always physically excited. On the other hand, a person in a fit of anger is excited, and that certainly is the opposite of love.

Unfortunately, too many of us limit troth to sex. For too many men love consists of sleeping with a woman, preferably endowed with curves, to whom they have acquired exclusive rights through marriage. Marriage—to use George Bernard Shaw's phrase—is nothing more than legalized prostitution. Males often regard their wives as sex-objects rather than persons. Such marriages are not likely to endure much longer than the curves that initiated the relationship. Understandably modern women rebel against being considered sex-objects. Their reaction is typical of the spirit of the times: let's turn the tables on men and make them objects to be used and discarded as we see fit. But renewing hostilities between the sexes is also futile.

When sexuality means only physical sexuality, and when we isolate it from the total person, two things can happen. We can make sex divine or we can allow it to become demonic. Actually, these two results belong together. Trying to achieve the divine forces us to follow sexual passions at any cost. We are driven by the demon of sex even as we grab for the goddess of sex. Denis de Rougemont has captured it well: "Eros . . . in ceasing to be a god, he ceases to be a demon."[3] Pascal made the same point about man in general: "Man is neither angel nor beast, the pity is that when he would make himself an angel, he makes himself a beast."[4]

Reducing troth and love to physical sexuality tears the meaning out of even physical sexuality. If orgasm is everything in life, then we must concentrate on getting bigger and better orgasms no matter what bizzare forms they take. Finally we run into meaninglessness, and even intercourse begins to be totally void of pleasure.

When a man and a woman engage in intercourse without giving themselves in mutual troth, they become initiates practicing the magic of demonized sex. They make futile attempts to get satisfaction by changing the scenery, experimenting with the erotic practices of tribal peoples, or stimulating the senses with aphrodisiacs and other erotica. Since they never make a personal surrender to their partner, they never achieve the ultimate orgasm. And so they roll from bed to bed like the characters in Henry Miller's novels, ever more frustrated and washed-out. In the words of Karl Barth, "Coitus without coexistence is demonic."[5]

Like any human act, sexual intercourse involves the full man; it is not just animal copulation added to human life. The physical, biotic, and psychic aspects of human activity are human and not animal. For human activity, in distinction from animal life, these aspects are foundational but not determinative. Biotic and psychic patterns keep animals together. In mortal combat a defeated wolf bares his jugular vein in surrender. But the victor does not slash it lest the species die out. Human communities, however, can't be held together simply with biotic and psychic patterns. Even though these patterns exist in men, they can destroy a community if they want to. Too often that's just what man has done when he pushed through for the jugular.

The difference between man and animals is also clear in mating. Animal copulation is immediately tied up with propagation and occurs according to rigidly patterned instincts. We have drives also—for food, comfort, physical intercourse, security, and so on. What we don't have are physical or psychic mechanisms that automatically come into play to satisfy these drives. We have physical sexual intercourse when we want to, not seasonally, at random, or out of glandular compulsion.

Although man's sexual drives are certainly involved, human intercourse depends on human choice and responsibility opened up by troth. Man decides to express his drives in one way or another. This possibility of making choices—whether right or wrong—is exclusively human. Thus, men find intercourse meaningful in the context of their full lives, not just in the reproductive cycle. Therefore, intercourse has the unique function of revealing and strengthening a particular bond of intimacy and fidelity between two people.

Physical Intercourse in Marriage

Intercourse between a man and a woman is qualitatively different from animal copulation. Furthermore, intercourse achieves its true purpose only in the bonds of marriage. The couple may protest that they love each other; yet intercourse without troth is always self-serving and a flight from responsibility. Intercourse itself is not self-serving or irresponsible, but isolating it from full personal commitment is.

31

Troth in marriage involves becoming "one body" in many ways—economic, aesthetic, psychic, educational, and political. At the same time, couples do not merge their personalities or devour each other. However, they must keep troth in all these areas, or the trust itself will tarnish. Their relationship will be severely strained if they cannot agree on financial priorities, if they can't consider and discuss important matters, if a husband deliberately flouts his wife's tastes, if a wife withholds her emotional support in tight situations, and so on.

However, unless a man and a woman seal these different levels of troth-intercourse with physical intercourse, their special relationship will not be as exclusive or intensive as it is meant to be. Their trust for each other is strengthened and deepened by physical intercourse. It is not true that a man's love for his wife is good but his physical desire for her is evil. This spiritualized love flowed from the mistaken notion that the soul is good and the body evil. Just the opposite is true: the love or troth in marriage is as deep and intense as it is because of its physical foundation. Troth pilots the physical intercourse; the physical intercourse deepens the troth. In that interaction a marriage grows in all its facets.

Physical intercourse is a good gift of the Lord in the marriage-room of the creation. And it ought to stay there if it is to be enjoyed freely. If sex-with-anyone becomes a principle rather than just a biological possibility, the partners inevitably experience elements of selfishness, exploitation, and insecurity. They seek the elusive apple of divine ecstasy only to have it turn into bitter fruit. Every man becomes a belligerent, and women learn to hate each other in the sexual war that allows only the best to survive. Even so-called free love breeds war between the sexes. The man or woman who does not score high on a performance scale is liable to be discarded like last year's shirt.

Despite the claims, there is no freedom here. There is only the growing fear of failure. Partners who fear failure become anxious and fretful—and they fail. Treating sex like something divine to be grabbed when the grabbing is good, turns it into a tyrant which unmercifully drives its slaves to try and try again. From behind all the froth and frenzy of modern "swingers" the same sad picture emerges. In a futile effort to escape this life-destroying syndrome, many (especially among the young) try to trivialize the whole matter. Intercourse is simply another physical need. A person needs a sandwich, a ball-point pen, and sex. It is as simple as that—and as terrifying.

Love in this context is no more love than it is free. Man becomes a slave of his passions on a level with the animals. His love is totally determined by occasional physical appetite. Sex-for-the-fun-of-it leads to sex-to-the-death-of-it.

Marriage, however, demythologizes sexual intercourse, stripping it of its pseudodivinity. A husband and wife discover that it is not divine; it is not the sweet mystery of life without which man cannot be happy. Marriage also takes the demon out of sexual intercourse. Man no longer has to struggle with the physical sex drive as if it were an evil tyrant demanding satisfaction from men and animals alike. Furthermore, marriage rehabilitates physical sexuality. Sex is not just a consumer activity in which one tries a man or woman as he tries out a ball-point pen. Sex is not candy. Within marriage physical intercourse is the culmination and seal of every level of bodily intercourse under the pledge of troth —the joyous, spontaneous, playful, complete, free giving of oneself to another person and the joyous, spontaneous, playful, complete, free receiving of another person to oneself.

Of course, I am not claiming that this kind of intercourse always happens in every marriage or even at all in some. We know better! I am saying that the conditions for having a good, joyful, free relationship are found only in marriage. Physical intercourse loses its created place when we indulge in it outside of marriage. Only in marriage can the couple work and demand the blessing of the Lord on their relationship, including intercourse.

Physical intercourse is only a fully human activity because it is qualified by troth (or the lack of troth). From one point of view, the same physical act occurs whenever two people have intercourse. Even the psychic elements look much alike from one intercourse to another.

33

However, when human sexuality is stripped of troth and restricted to the physical and the psychic dimensions, people can argue that "marriage" and "adultery" are meaningless categories. The sex-for-the-fun-of-it mentality champions this view: it's more or less all the same anyway—physical intercourse plus or minus fun. We can only distinguish between fornication, adultery, incest, rape, and conjugal love if human physical intercourse is a total act which can only take place because of God's Word of troth for marriage. Without the norm of troth we could not say whether a specific act of intercourse was conjugal love or adultery. Under the norm of troth, though, the matter clears up: intercourse that occurs under the leading of pledged troth is married love, but intercourse that fails to live up to the troth norm is self-serving adultery.

Troth Is Not Romance

Every marriage needs romantic feeling, but it should not be confused with troth. Although romantic congeniality usually draws two people together, romantic feelings by themselves are too capricious and uncertain to serve as the dominant factor in marriage. Man's psychic swings between periods of tension and relaxation would make a marriage built on psychic feeling (mistakenly called love by many) an on-again, off-again business. What's more, marriage could be on-again, off-again with several partners since everyone is psychically attracted to any number of people. No wonder Emil Brunner considered a marriage based on love or romance to be doomed from the outset. "To base marriage on love is to build on the sand."[6]

Not every night in marriage is like the wedding night. Even with the artificial stimulation of American advertising and love-potions, no one can maintain constant romance throughout his marriage. Partners who believe that sentiment is everything have a most difficult time. The wife may begin to ask the question: "Is he really right for me? He doesn't turn me on like he used to; the magic touch is gone." She may compare the advantages and disadvantages of her marriage with the possibility of a new relationship. Or she may try desperately to maintain her sex appeal, whether for her husband or for someone else. As Margaret Mead reports, the wife is likely to take out her curlers and put on fresh lipstick before waking up her husband in the morning. In that kind of marriage the norm is no longer troth, but whether or not the partners are still exciting to each other.

Instead of counting on each other as faithful partners, the husband and wife feel the constant tension of knowing they may lose out to someone else. The wife must be sensuous enough to keep her husband at a low level of excitement. He must be daring, aggressive, and sensuous himself. But physical attractiveness and personal success are uncertain at best and almost inevitably wane.

Although a marriage does not revolve around congeniality, a marriage without it is sad. Couples that develop a deep emotional intimacy will find their compatibility growing, adding spice and vigor to their relationship.[7] All marriages benefit from tenderness, expressiveness, affection, as well as romantic moments of intense feeling. It also helps to understand and adjust to each other's moods.

Fostering Intimacy

A husband and wife who work at fostering intimacy and troth should not wipe out individual differences and become as much alike as possible. By no means. Neither do they need to agree on everything or have the same likes and dislikes. What they must agree on is the basic meaning of their marriage.

Troth thrives on the uniqueness of the individuals in the relation. Partners who feel threatened and do not allow each other their own expectations, feelings, and identity do not really have troth. A compulsive, clinging-vine attachment that leaves no room for growth is as unhealthy as an arrangement in which two people exist together without any inner contact or commitment. In both cases there really is no relationship because each partner treats the other as an extension of himself. Forgetting his partner is a real person, he smothers his spouse. Regrettably, such situations are quite common, especially where wives have been told that submission means self-abdication and self-erasure. Such misreading of the Scriptures has caused untold agony for many women who have felt guilty not only for resisting this kind of submission but especially for harboring deep feelings of hostility against the husband and the God that demanded it. They feel unhappy about being unhappy. Yet more and more they experience marriage as a life-sentence to boredom and frustration. In the past a considerable number of women seem to have found a way to make a life of complying with their husbands' every wish. Today, people ask for more vibrancy, depth, and sharing in marriage, and fewer women can last an entire lifetime as a half-person.

Although at times it may seem easier to let one partner take over, a husband and wife can jeopardize their entire relation by establishing a male-dominated marriage. When a woman virtually surrenders her personality to her husband, she has less to give to the relationship as the years pass. Outwardly she may seem rather content, but inwardly she grows more and more dependent until she is only an adjunct. Often powerful feelings of hostility well up inside her, against herself for succumbing and against her husband (and God) for demanding such subservience. She feels her marriage is a "trap" with four walls and a husband as keeper.

The situation becomes more complicated when the husband continues to grow through outside contacts while the wife languishes at home. He may have begun to grow away from her when he promised to keep his office problems out of the home. Unfortunately, after years of living separate lives, he may begin to feel that his wife no longer has the understanding to be his confidante and equal. Despite her dutiful obedience and continual adoration, he begins to see her as an embarrassment. Sometimes, feeling guilty, he pampers her even more (just the wrong thing if he wants her to grow up); at other times he suddenly drops her for "no apparent reason," using her childish behavior (accentuated by his pampering) to justify an affair.

A relationship of mutual respect can only grow and deepen between two persons who each have an identity. They need to know that beyond being husband and wife, they are man and woman. Being a husband or a wife does not exhaust each partner's personality. Both of them also need other relationships with friends, colleagues, fellow artists, business partners. Such legitimate relations should stimulate the marriage, not compete with it. A man and woman need to be sure that they do not overburden their marriage in an effort to satisfy all their needs. It cannot bear the strain. Partners can seek and receive various kinds of satisfaction from other relationships without endangering their marriage. In fact, as long as they live in the knowledge that marriage is for the two of them, all these other contacts will only add to the health, zest, and intimacy of the marriage.

Everyone needs to respect his mate as a person to develop a healthy relation. In each other a couple experiences warmth and acceptance, encouragement and ebullience, trust and esteem. They also find restraint and correction, empathy and understanding. Both husband and wife become stronger people in the invigorating steadiness and dependability of such troth. Their self-esteem grows, making them more able to cope with their tasks. Deep troth increases their resiliency in dark times and their verve and confidence in good times.

In troth neither husband nor wife will try to manipulate the other by threatening to leave or by refusing intercourse until he or she meets certain conditions. Unless the two of them grow together out of mutual self-respect their marriage will be a charade with less and less depth and satisfaction every year. Couples who support each other in crises deepen their relationship, but couples who can't support each other under pressure are pulled even farther apart.

Soap opera wives can pout and complain that their husbands don't understand them or take them seriously. We put up with that sort of thing on TV, but in a real-life marriage such complaints are much more serious than the simplistic plot elements of TV. Real troth cannot grow unless both husband and wife try to understand each other, to take each other seriously, and to accept each other as equally important people.

Only couples who understand and accept each other can open themselves up to the deep sharing that germinates the plant of troth and makes it grow.

Even children feel insulted when we respond to their stories with an "uh-huh" or "That's nice, sweetheart." The "good listener" we admire so much probably gets so many invitations because so few people have anyone who really listens to them. Even in marriage listening is difficult because it forces us to reveal ourselves and even to invest ourselves in the other person; yet it is indispensable if troth is to flourish. A husband or wife who opens up to his partner can be deeply hurt if he gets only a hearing when he really needed understanding. Nothing is as demoralizing or as unnerving as pouring out his heart in confidence and then discovering that the other person is not with him, not really understanding, and perhaps even manipulating him. He reached for intimacy, but he came away feeling vulnerable and exploited, as well as sad and insecure. No wonder he avoids opening himself up, and no wonder deep troth never develops.

Negative and Positive Troth-Cycles

Couples caught in this alarming pattern soon discover that it is both debilitating and self-perpetuating: one partner feels misunderstood and hurt, therefore he grows wary of opening up. As he falls back on himself, he can no longer listen to others. When he misunderstands them, they hesitate to respond to him; and finally, after going through the cycle numerous times, he finds himself shut in to complete loneliness. This negative cycle of intimidation, retreat, and final immobilization is powerful but it can be broken by the concern and understanding of troth. Sometimes, though, the fears that feed this cycle are deeply rooted in the person's psyche and in his past. If so, he may need special psychotherapeutic counseling, guided by the troth norm, to expose and dispel his fears.

Married couples will find that a positive troth-cycle is self-reinforcing and exhilarating. They are understood; therefore they open up. Consequently, they cope so well with themselves and with growing that they can even reach out to other people. They learn to understand others and to experience communion. Finally, after going through the cycle many times, they discover that they've built a relationship of deep troth based on mutual respect and self-esteem.

Intimacy of this kind is not easy. And in today's world it is even more difficult than in some periods of the past. Even though we risk being misunderstood, we need to learn to pull each other out of negative intimidation-retreat cycles and back into healthy understanding-liberation cycles. That task demands closeness, which means people must open up to each other. Although all people need such intimacy, many fear it because they are afraid to reveal who they really are. In fact, they often are much less wary about physical nakedness.

If a husband and wife are to remain open to each other, they should explore together areas of difficulty until each can understand the other's point of view. Each needs to make sure he is really hearing what the other is saying instead of what he wants to hear. We easily misread each other because our real meanings are so often quite different from what the flow of words indicates.

Sometimes a husband unwittingly says something that touches his wife on a sore point, and she thinks he is accusing her. Feeling exposed and unable to cope, she flares up with "What do you know about it?" or "None of your business!" The husband feels hurt and misreads his wife's response. When both feel accused, it's little wonder that they react with, "OK, if that's the way you want it, two can play the game!" And that ends that discussion. A little understanding and some care in reading each other right would help prevent such misunderstandings between people who basically love each other.

Couples who have a growing troth relation will be less likely to misread each other simply because neither partner needs devious ways to express what he has on his mind. He can say it straight without attacking the other person. Beating around the bush, as we say, gets us into trouble because no one knows what we really mean. Once we foster an aura of mistrust in the minds of others, we have a hard time shaking it. On the other hand, all of us know a person who speaks so straight that we feel we can trust him. Mutual respect grows, and we find ourselves in a positive troth-cycle.

Only Troth Means Freedom

If marriage partners do not consider their relation a permanent trust for life, they will live in permanent crisis. If a person marries, as many do today, thinking that a breakup will provide away out if it doesn't work, the marriage will in all likelihood end up in the divorce courts. If partners regard the "freedom" to leave as a real option, it becomes a specter that haunts the marriage. As a result the husband and wife cannot achieve the real freedom they need to develop authentic troth. Only within the bonds of troth is a marriage really free.

Marriage has to be a betrothal for life, or the partners will never be able to tolerate quarreling, arguing, sulking, mistakes, disagreements, or even the mildest criticism. All conflicts become traumatic experiences, for over every quarrel hangs these unsettling questions: Do I want a divorce now? Does she want out? Is he trying to get rid of me? Every time the quarrel ends, they must reestablish their mutual pledge, but the tension of such a major decision dogs the marriage. Slowly partners learn to put off decisions, to avoid arguments at all costs, and to maintain only superficial contacts. Eventually the marriage disintegrates. The partners have no freedom because they have never settled the most basic matter in their marriage. Only couples who pledge their troth for life have the freedom to develop their marriage as they should. Only such marriages can really survive and indeed flourish in the midst of problems and even arguments. Only dead or dying marriages have no conflict. Couples who are not sure of their bonds of troth avoid differences and confrontations at all costs. Their marriages sink into colorlessness and gradually drift toward breakdown. One sad day the partners wake up and discover that the troth relationship doesn't exist. One so-called solution is an affair; another is divorce.

Clearly, genuine troth also rules out the modern phenomenon of trial marriage. Indeed, a trial marriage is a contradiction in terms. According to the norm, any relationship which the partners consider a test or trial is not a marriage. To take a marriage vow is to say, "We are in it together for life." A trial marriage, then, is not a good "trial" for marriage because it lacks the essential ingredients of stability and permanence.

Open Marriage

The mutual commitment of troth is also the key element missing in the discussion of "open marriage."[8] Honesty and openness in marriage, deep sharing and concern are obviously desirable, as this discussion has indicated. But to talk about emotional openness and congeniality in marriage without troth is to talk about the cart without the horse. Without troth to give the freedom and context, a man and a woman will withdraw from their freedom to be open for fear that complete honesty might destroy their relationship. A man and a woman can only gradually share more of their real selves when they know their partner will stand by in all circumstances. Openness without troth is like sinking sand: one never knows when he will be pulled under.

Certainly psychic openness deepens the intimacy of troth in marriage. If, however, we treat such openness as the cardinal mark of marriage, we are in just as much trouble as if we say marriage is basically romance. If openness is the touchstone of marriage, any relationship of real sharing and loving concern is basically no different than marriage. We are now faced with the following unpleasant dilemma: either we accept affairs as the inevitable result of being honest and "open" (the conclusion, which many draw from the discussion of open marriage) or we vainly struggle to keep up our guard and avoid genuine, intimate contact with anyone other than our spouses, thus burdening the marriage with the impossible task of being all things to all men. Only in troth can we avoid this dilemma and build a genuinely open marriage.

NOTES

1. Lionel Tiger and Robin Fox, *The Imperial Animal* (New York: Holt, Rinehart and Winston, 1971).

2. See Appendix for discussion of this matter in regard to the Pauline writings.

3. Denis de Rougement, *Love in the Western World* (New York: Pantheon, 1956), p. 312.

4. Blaise Pascal, *Pensées* VII, 258 (London: Harvill Press, 1962), p. 173.

5. Karl Barth, *Church Dogmatics* III/4 (Edinburgh: T & T Clark, 1961), p. 133.

6. Emil Brunner, *The Divine Imperative* (London: Lutterworth Press, 1937), p. 345.

7. *The Intimate Marriage* by Howard J. Clinebell, Jr., and Charlotte H. Clinebell (New York: Harper and Row, 1970) is excellent for all who reach for deepened emotional intimacy.

8. Nena O'Neill and George O'Neill, *Open Marriage* (New York: J. B. Lippincott, 1972).

3

MARRIAGE: COURTSHIP, CEREMONY, AND BREAKDOWN

In today's troubled, lonely, complex world, marriage is as important as it ever was. In marriage man and wife can be at ease with each other, admit mistakes, nourish each other's needs, enjoy each other's company, share confidences, be healed together. Their relationship can enrich and strengthen them to take up other tasks in the kingdom.

Although marriage is every bit as important as it ever was, it is more vulnerable to attack than ever before, largely because it lacks the support which surrounded it in earlier times. Modern marriages are not linked by patrimonies, with their indissoluble law, kinship ties, and socioeconomic pressures. Even family considerations are no longer as strong as in the past when marriages stayed together for the sake of the children. A man does not need a woman to cook, do the laundry, care for the children, or make the beds. He can go to a restaurant, call a laundry, hire a governess, or go to a hotel. A woman, in turn, need not stay at home waiting for the husband to bring home his paycheck. She can get a job and bring home her own paycheck. Physical satisfaction is also more and more separated from the bonds of marriage, especially since technology has removed the triple curse of conception, detection, and infection.

Previously, nonethical motivations—safety, economics, class, prestige, religion, and so on—were the weighty considerations in a marriage. The patriarchal structure of society was often even more important because people thought marriage was a matter of the tribe or at least the extended family.

Today, all these considerations are less important. In addition, most people choose a marriage partner on the basis of personal preferences. Unfortunately, even preferences vary from time to time. Today's marriage has nothing to depend on but troth. A marriage today has to make it as a marriage—a union of troth—or it does not make it at all.

No wonder, then, that modern marriages are in trouble. We know little or nothing about troth because we've allowed it to shrink to mere physical fidelity. Since a man and woman can have sex with each other without being married, we no longer know what to make of marriage. So many couples are unaware of a deeper troth (and the social scientists who try to guide them are just as ignorant as their students) that marriage is on the rocks and slipping fast. This kind of situation has always existed, of course, but the effects were neither as widespread nor as widely known because partners tended to stay together even without deep bonds of troth. Although external reasons still keep some marriages intact, fewer and fewer people are putting up with each other for these reasons alone.

Interestingly enough, this also means that the skyrocketing divorce rates are somewhat deceptive. Not only are more and more marriages failing, but it is true that fewer and fewer couples are hiding their marital breakdown. In fact, many young people are cynical about marriage because of the past practice of remaining together even when the heart of a marriage had been cut out.

Marriage and Family

Although the relationship between a man and a woman is often intertwined with their relationship to the family, we should not confuse the two. Each relationship has its own unique structure. A childless couple is not a family or even an incomplete family as many have thought; it is simply a marriage. Yet within a family the marriage relationship remains distinct, or at least it ought to.

The offices of husband and wife differ from the parental office. Since a man and a woman usually occupy both offices, overlappings are inevitable; yet somehow the couple needs to maintain the distinction between their roles. For instance, children normally address their mother as mom, while husbands normally address their wives by their first name or some term of endearment such as *love, honey, darling.* Sometimes a husband also addresses his wife as mom to teach the children that the woman who cares for them is their mother. There is nothing wrong with that, of course, but a husband who always calls his wife mom in adult company or when alone together may be suggesting that he needs a mother more than a wife! Certainly the husband's name for his wife reflects on how they understand their relationship. Similarly, when children learn to know their father and mother as Ted and Alice, we recognize their understanding of family relations.

The distinction between marriage roles and family roles has important implications. For one, we cannot define marriage as a means of procreation. God has made marriages serviceable for the beginning of families; in fact, couples usually find their marriage is enriched through interrelation with families. Nevertheless, marriage is first of all for the partners —for their mutual enrichment, enjoyment, fellowship, and growth. It was harder to distinguish the marriage function in earlier times when the family was the productive, consumptive, cultic, political, educational, affectional, protective, and socializing unit. However, today's less encumbered family allows couples to see their own relationship more clearly.

Nearly everyone today distinguishes the school, church, business, and state from the family. It is time that we also pay more attention to the difference between marriage and family. With relatively easy family planning and less demanding families, a marriage relationship today can more easily live its own life.

If the husband-wife relationship is unique, the partners must set aside time to foster and deepen their relationship. Too often a husband and wife are only engrossed in each other during physical intercourse. The rest of the time they relate to each other as parents or as church members or whatever. Each partner needs to learn that his wife or husband deserves and needs time if the two of them are to understand each other better and deepen their intimacy. If they can't give each other time with joy and spontaneity, their troth relation will begin to sputter, boredom will set in, and even physical intercourse will suffer. An affair is just around the corner. In our day this task is even more crucial than ever, for today's marriage survives and grows strong by the slender thread of troth, or it flounders and dies as the troth frazzles and breaks.

Neither Basically a Legal nor an Ecclesiastical Institution

Understanding marriage as a union of troth is also endangered because many of us are still tempted to look for the basis of marriage in the law or in the church's sanction. However, neither the marriage license from the state nor the blessing of the church makes a marriage what it is: a moral bond of troth between two people who marry each other before the Lord.

God's plan makes marriage serviceable for beginning a family. Still, a marriage is not primarily a legal institution whose "essence" is its natural purpose of procreation, as traditional Thomist doctrine held. Whether we think of it sacramentally or legally, marriage is not a "remedy for sin" either. Even if sanctioned by civil or canon law, a marriage is not a contractual legal agreement giving two persons the right to each other's body. Marriage is simply marriage; it is not a part of the state or the church. For much of the modern era marriage has been a football kicked back and forth between state and church. Even today the matter has not really been settled since most of us still conceive of marriage largely in legal or ecclesiastical terms.

For ancient peoples marriage was a sacred event.[1] For the early Romans marriage meant that the woman was transferred from her father's religion to her bridegroom's. However, between the seventh and fifth centuries B.C., social institutions—including marriage—were gradually dissociated from their religious foundations. People began to marry because they felt drawn to each other. At the very beginning of the Christian era in imperial Rome men and women married without any kind of legal procedure; they simply agreed to marry. In the sixth century Emperor Justinian declared: *"nuptias non concubitus, sed consensus facit"* (marriage is not made by intercourse, but by consent, *Digesta* XXXV, I, 15). Although the authority of the priests and of the state was real, it actually had nothing to do with the essential act of marriage because people considered it a personal and family matter. It was not until the time of the Roman Empire that a marriage document, the *tabulae nuptiales*, was introduced from the East.

In the early Christian church also, marriage was a personal and family matter, protected by the statutes of the realm. Although the community of believers was always concerned about marriage, we have no evidence of priestly prayer and blessing on marriages until the fourth century. Even then the ecclesiastical ceremonies that developed were optional, even external to the marriage contracted civilly within the family. As late as the ninth century Pope Nicholas I still considered marriages by mutual consent valid even if civil, family, and church ceremonies were not performed.

It was not until the eleventh and twelfth centuries that the church obtained complete jurisdiction over marriage, including the contract and civil aspects. By the thirteenth century, marriage had become a sacrament. The Reformation brought the end of the church's jurisdiction and a public reaction against marriage's sacramental character. Marriage became a matter between a man and a woman whom the church ought to bless. In Protestant countries marriage legislation reverted to the state, even though people still thought of marriage as a divine institution.

The French Revolution saw the beginning of the civil marriage proper. The Constitution of 1791 stated that marriage was only a civil contract established by means of civil act. Throughout the nineteenth century the state increasingly took to itself the right to establish marriages. In many countries at present a man and woman may choose between a civil or an ecclesiastical rite, both making the marriage legally valid.

From a distance of several centuries, two problems stand out. First, in the early centuries of the Christian era, believers sensed the importance of mutual commitment in marriage. However, they appear to have inherited it from their Roman past rather than from Christian reflection based on the Scriptures. This was a weak basis for defending marriage from the sharp attacks it suffered. In the midst of the turmoil, Christians resorted to polemic defense rather than deep reflection. Perhaps that is why they gradually allowed the meaning of marriage to focus more and more on its civil regulation and its ecclesiastical confirmation. Furthermore, when the Reformers denied the sacramental character of marriage, they unwittingly strengthened the state's hold on marriage until the time when the spirit of the French Revolution made an entrenchment of the civil character of marriage quite easy.

Even today wedding ceremonies suggest a lingering confusion. Many churches offer couples a choice between a "private" wedding (the minister acts as a "servant of the state") and a "church" wedding (the minister leads in an official worship service). Some insist on "church" weddings because they fear a civil ceremony will depreciate or endanger the covenantal character of marriage. Others prefer "private" weddings because they see the "church" wedding as a lamentable remnant of the church's pre-Reformation control. Each group makes an important point.

Clearly, marriage needs to come into its own as a creation of the Lord differing from the communities of worship and justice. Only then can we emphasize the God-given, holy character of marriage without allowing it to be absorbed by the church. Only when marriage is basically independent of both church and state can we define the proper relations between the three institutions.

Marriage and the State

The state's primary concern with marriage is to safeguard it against as many outside encroachments and pressures as possible. Healthy marriages are important to a well-functioning state, but the state must also protect the couple and their potential family by maintaining certain minimum conditions with mandatory blood tests and laws against bigamy, and so forth. Thus, the modern state issues marriage licenses as a safeguard for the couple beginning life in a complex society. These licenses are the state's legal recognition that two people have given themselves to each other in marriage. By issuing the license the state pledges to do all it can to promote conditions which will be for its good. At the same time, the state informs the couple that it will hereafter hold the couple responsible for living up to the vows which they have voluntarily taken.

Although the state itself should not become a marriage counselor, as part of its pledge to protect the integrity of the marriage, it should make sure genuine marriage counseling is available for marriages in crisis. In fact the state should help each faith-community within its jurisdiction to have its own marriage counseling service.

Even the best of states falls far short of such a goal, but then, so do couples with the best intentions. Sometimes a marriage dies in spite of the support and encouragement of the state and other parts of society. In such situations the state can only acknowledge that the marriage is dead and issue a writ of divorce. The state is responsible to see if the couple received any kind of help before deciding a reconciliation was out of the question.

Marriage and the Church

The church is also vitally concerned that a marriage be in the Lord because its mandate to preach the Word of God is for all of life. The church holds God's command and promise of troth before a couple. It then calls every couple to confess that they find joy in this Word of God and that their marriage can only find root in Jesus Christ. In turn, the community of believers promises to do everything possible to support the marriage. That support makes both marriages and churches thrive because a worship community is only as vibrant and healthy as its members. The minister's role is not to marry the couple but to acknowledge that God himself marries them in their vowed promise of troth.

From time to time the church must remind its married members of their vows and responsibilities. It also needs to bring healing to couples whose marriages are breaking down. Pastors and elders who counsel will be tempted to be judgmental and punitive, especially with a man and woman who are outwardly indifferent to their situation. Counselors may find it a little easier to be patient and understanding with a couple who are overwhelmed with guilt and a sense of failure. However, condemnation doesn't help either kind of couple. The first pair is likely to grow defensive rather than penitent; the second already feels condemned. Counselors can accomplish more by helping the partners themselves face up to their problems and discover ways to rebuild and heal. Counselors also need to foster openness, concern, understanding, trust, and authenticity. While the church must be firm in maintaining the norm for marriage, it must also show sympathy for those who have a hard time living up to it. A firm counselor can still show empathy without approving of the situation. In fact, the counselor who firmly maintains the norm with empathy and genuine love shapes the setting in which a couple can more easily admit their shortcomings and accept the guidance of the norm.

The Wedding Ceremony

A wedding ceremony is a feast of celebration in which two people stop their regular routine to think about the meaning of the new life they are about to begin together. One of the best ways to commemorate the change taking place in their lives is to celebrate with people from all areas of life. Since their marriage is not the only relationship the couple has, they take their vows before parents, other family members, friends, the state, and the church. The invited "guests"—whether individuals or institutions—are all vitally concerned with the new marriage because the couple will only be able to carry out their other responsibilities in society if their marriage is reasonably healthy. And so, the wedding ceremony actually has two sides to it. On the one hand, the couple makes their pledge of troth publicly and asks for the encouragement, support, and blessing of their guests and of society in general. On the other hand, each part of society present reminds the couple of the requirements for marriage. If the couple agrees to these requirements, the guests—parents, family, friends, state, and church—offer their blessing and pledge their support for the marriage.

This kind of ceremony stresses the couple's *public* pledge of mutual troth. Couples who believe in Christ will confess their troth before fellow believers in response to the Word of God for marriage. In fact, the wedding ceremony can give concrete form to the various pledges involved. For instance, parents can publicly give their consent and approval as evidence of God's faithfulness from generation to generation. Friends and relatives can express their joy and witness the pledge. The bridal party will no longer be basically decorative. Instead, the men and women can fit into the ceremony as witnesses, who act on behalf of friends and acquaintances to acknowledge publicly their responsibility to respect and support the marriage. When the couple, the witnesses, and the minister sign the papers, they signify that they've met the legal requirements for marriage. Throughout this public ritual, the minister pledges the church's support. In this ceremonial way a marriage is born.

The ritual in this kind of wedding service reminds everyone present that the meaning of marriage is rooted in Jesus Christ and his kingdom of righteousness and peace. The couple confesses that their hope and joy is in the Word of God for marriage. Then they begin their life together by formally relating their marriage to other parts of God's kingdom and by formally asking for support and encouragement from these areas. Once they are assured that outside matters are in order, the couple is free to be engrossed in each other and fully enjoy their intimacy in troth. After the solemn vows, it is time to rejoice and celebrate what the Lord has done in the lives of the bride and groom. The feast ought to be a natural outcome of the ceremony itself. The couple celebrates the joy of troth with their family and friends. Guests raise toasts, assuring each other of continued support. With joy and laughter the guests celebrate the hope accompanying the marriage.

Marriage without a License

Marriage ceremonies have come under some deserved attack lately. Many young couples reject the common idea that a marriage license "makes" the marriage. Therefore, they refuse to apply for state confirmation of their marriages, maintaining that the quality of the relationship is what counts. In some circles strong public censure only convinces the young people that the older generation stays together because of the law rather than because of any genuine relationship.

Obviously, these young couples are right on at least one count. A marriage license does not make a marriage; it only registers the fact that the state recognizes the birth of a new marriage. However, a marriage license also obligates the state to look out for the couple's welfare, to protect them and their family in a society of complex interlacements.

Couples who resist legalization of their marriage should be listened to sympathetically. If they want to avoid considering their relationship basically legal and civil, they are certainly on the right track. However, some will still refuse a license even after the civil aspect of marriage is put in its proper limited place. For these couples the license is not the real problem. If their relationship is so strong, intimate, and real, why not make it public? Sometimes the fuss about the license hides an uncertainty about the nature of the relationship itself. The couple may not really be sure that they are ready to commit themselves to each other for life. In effect, they are opting for "trial" marriage with all the built-in uncertainties we discussed earlier.

A genuine marriage can only grow strong when it receives the recognition and respect of society as a whole. Since marriage does not stand in isolation, it cannot grow and develop as it should if it is continually turned in upon itself. If a couple keeps their "marriage" secret, no one can recognize and respect it. Consequently, no one leaves space for it to be and grow. Friends are at a loss as to how to treat the couple. Parents are embarrassed by what seems obvious although no one publicly acknowledges it. If they do not make their relationship public in various ways, the man and woman will find themselves under unbearable pressures. Their marriage will become overburdened and artificial. Eventually, it will disintegrate. The artificiality which we all feel in relation to a couple that keeps nothing private is just as real as the artificiality of a couple that makes nothing public. Such secrecy implies that the couple sees something wrong with their relationship. When a troth relationship matures to the point of total commitment to each other, it needs full public acknowledgment to be integrated into society. If the man and woman keep the relationship secret, even if only from the state, their marriage cannot achieve the full identity necessary for integration.

Premarital Intercourse

Many people claim premarital intercourse is no longer an issue in America. However, it is still enough of an issue to provide conflicts for soap operas and movies. What's more, it is an important issue to the girl who finds herself unmarried and pregnant. Actually, the term itself misses the point because it focuses on intercourse before or after the ceremony, a distinction that is simplistic and misguided, if not wrong. Strictly speaking, two people who pledge troth and seal it with physical intercourse are married. At the same time, since public acknowledgment is part of the marital pledge of troth, they are anticipating what is not yet rightly theirs. They should be urged to make it public as soon as possible. However, two people who have intercourse outside of the mutual commitment of troth need to learn that they are playing with fire—and should stop before they burn themselves even more. In a real sense, there is no such thing as premarital intercourse. For a man and woman who have not officially married, there are only two kinds of relations: intercourse in a marriage which has not yet come into its own, or intercourse which has nothing to do with marriage at all. The difference is crucial even though few recognize it. The basic point is not whether the couple had a valid license when they had intercourse, but whether the intercourse took place in mutual troth. The ceremony and the license are important aspects of the marriage in making the relationship public, but the troth meaning is central.

If an unmarried couple admit that they've had intercourse (with or without resulting pregnancy), they must not simply be expected to go through a marriage ceremony. Whether or not they legalize their relationship ought to depend entirely on the nature and quality of their troth. The so-called shotgun wedding tries to make a marriage where no marriage exists. To force the couple to legalize their relationship when they have no troth only compounds the problem. Fortunately, some couples find that troth develops, and a real marriage gradually evolves. Just as often, however, the couple is doomed to a lifelong relation of indifference and misery.

We accomplish very little by sternly admonishing young people to abstain until they have gone through the official ceremony. We really need to stress the fact that physical intercourse is a precious experience which should be shared only in deep troth. Only then can it express and strengthen authenticity and integrity. In this context, we recognize the importance of physical intercourse, but we do not focus on it at the expense of the troth relation.

Courtship and Dating

We may like to think that marriage comes naturally to everyone with normal emotions and sex drives. In fact, young people need more prepa-

54

ration for marriage today than ever before because of the heavy attacks on marriage and because of our modern obsession with physical sexuality. In general, the home, school, and church have the task of guiding young people into the kind of mature responsibility that will enable them to take up their various tasks in God's kingdom. Part of that guidance is troth education. The home, of course, should be a living example of troth. The church should proclaim that marriage is rooted in Jesus Christ, and the school should explore the meaning of marriage and family in a structured way, as communities of troth.

Gradually the family, school, and church help the young person grow in his awareness of the biblical meaning of marriage. Later when a couple are planning marriage, they should be able to turn to the Christian community for intense personal discussion. In fact, the church could take the lead in offering help since it ought to be aware of the kind of marriage it will be pledging to support.

Over the centuries men developed many patterns for selecting mates, but none of them prefigured our modern practice of allowing a single girl to go out alone with a young man. In earlier, relatively stable societies parents selected suitable mates, or a young man chose a wife from among the circle of friends he had come to know at chaperoned evenings in the family parlor or meetings at church. Before the 1920s a young man and a young woman were very seldom alone together.

In this century, however, the Western custom of dating is almost a necessity. With both men and women moving freely and with the population growing so rapidly, the young meet large numbers of people whom they might marry. Dating allows them something a bit better than random exposure. Dating's three stages—random dating, going steady, engagement—offer young people a chance to locate and evaluate each other personally before committing themselves to one mate.

No doubt, dating has many advantages. For instance, young people can come to know each other personally and then freely choose a partner. However, anyone who has dated much knows that it is often a highly manipulative and exploitative game with only one rule: give some to get more. Often the players become extremely competitive, struggling for prestige and popularity. Girls develop a practiced coyness to intrigue and entice. They play dumb and practice deceit in order to keep the fellows they want. Boys develop a bravado to seduce and thrill as many admiring girls as possible. They play the he-man so they can get the sexiest of the girls whenever they want them. The whole battle plan, complete with maneuvers of sexual offense and defense, is carefully disguised with talk of romance, love, and moonlight.

Marriage is certain to suffer from such a system because real troth has no place in it. Marriages resulting from such games often settle at the level of prostitution: wife plies husband and he pays. No wonder many husbands and wives who played by the rules of the game do not really know each other when they get married and the masks come off.

Fortunately, some young people are making serious efforts to avoid the sex-and-fun style of courtship. They say that dating only helped them know each other at a theater, on the beach, or over a meal someone else cooked. In their leisure activities, they could hide their real selves behind a carefully constructed mask of confidence and security. Even though they did not really know each other, they might be tempted to marry when their families applied a little pressure or when their fear of rejection or loneliness grew too great.

Lean-to Marriages

Couples who marry to fill an emotional need have as poor a basis for marriage as those who marry for prestige, money, thrills, or sexual satisfaction. Sometimes two insecure people marry, unaware that their emotional needs are dovetailing. One longs for warmth and tenderness which the other gives as a way of gaining acceptance and attention. Both think their union is safe. He gets all the warmth he wants without really having to commit himself; she is accepted without really having to face her neurotic need for it. Neither partner foresees the serious problems facing them.

Although the man and the woman meet each other's needs superficially, they are not really good for each other. And without help, their relationship will be shaky. At some point the husband will feel smothered by the woman's attention. He will grow edgy, feeling too crowded to grow. In turn, the wife will become upset and begin to doubt that she is accepted.

Often an outgoing, talkative fellow attracts a quiet introverted girl (or vice versa) because he seems to exude the qualities she lacks, confidence and self-esteem. Ironically, he is attracted to her for the same reason. She obviously has real confidence and self-esteem not to need a smokescreen of words behind which to hide. Each is seeking certainty and stability in the other.

The problems begin when the mates recognize that the other is not the confident, secure person which had been imagined. In fact, both feel worthless and rejected. However, often unable really to face up to this, husband and wife feel the compulsion to portray the ideal image the partner expects. This in turn reflects on the marriage because both partners, fearing exposure, avoid deep intimacy. The lean-to marriage is often at bottom an arm's-length marriage.

If there is a more or less open admittance of the deep insecurity, the couple can slowly grow together and fully support each other. However, often such relationships involve families and lives in a continual state of disarray. Moreover, if one of the partners matures and stands upright, the other partner most often falls hard. He or she wants or needs a "leaning" partner. At best such a marriage can only limp along; often it falls apart completely. Ideally the "leaning" (but now "falling") partner should be helped to stand up. Even then their marriage is very risky, for they must build a whole new relationship. Yet the initial attraction —their mutual need for confidence and security—is gone. The two "new" people in the marriage may or may not find each other compatible and congenial.

Marriage and Self-Image

The partners in a lean-to marriage (and many other types, for that matter) are likely to tell each other, "If I'd known what you were really like, I'd never have married you!" They realize they should have been serious about their courtship, honestly trying to know each other. For all couples, a major obstacle in developing troth and intimacy is their lack of self-knowledge. Only when a person knows himself well can he really meet and share with others.

As hard as some couples might try to know each other, they can't because each is projecting a façade of the person he thinks the other wants to marry. All of us feel uncertain of ourselves at one time or another, but couples who marry while still in search of themselves are in deep trouble. If we are not really in touch with ourselves, how can we be in touch with another person? Intimacy is almost impossible if we cannot accept ourselves, if we think we aren't worth much, or if we aren't even sure what kind of person we are. Knowing and accepting ourselves gives us self-assurance and stability. Without it we avoid problem situations and read every comment as proof that we are unloved and rejected. When we expect rejection, we ask for it, making it all the more difficult for others to accept us for what we are.

Mixed Marriages

We used to talk a great deal about the dangers of "mixed marriages." No one uses that term much anymore. In fact, many parents seem relieved just to see their children through a ceremony with almost anyone. Admittedly, the old discussion of mixed marriage missed the point by asking if a Baptist could marry a Lutheran or a Catholic could marry a Presbyterian. Yet a marriage between two people with different visions of life's meaning—the true mixed marriage—is a serious matter.

During courtship couples need to decide together what vision of life will permeate their life together. The basic vision they agree to will guide them in setting their priorities, in balancing their responsibilities, in making the day-to-day decisions. Unless a couple settles this basic question before their marriage, trouble is almost inevitable.

A marriage can only move successfully in one direction. If each partner follows a competing vision of life, their troth will never deepen. In fact, a shared vision is so important that a marriage of professed atheists or dedicated Communists is more likely to grow and deepen than a mixed marriage between a Christian and a non-Christian or a Communist and a Muslim. Still, some couples decide to leave it to chance or romantic love. They're likely to say something like, "I just know it will work out! We are so much in love!" Some try praying that it will turn out for the best, but do not work it through. Either way, they will be in for a rude shock and much heartache. Mutual commitment that is not rooted in the same understanding of life and marriage is extremely shaky. In the end either a biblical or an unbiblical vision of life guides the marriage and roots the commitment.

The Kingdom Vision

The importance of this matter for young people cannot be overestimated. Unless it is rooted in Christ, a couple's vision will take a part of creation and live as if it were everything. Whatever choice they make involves difficulties. For instance, they may choose to make marriage their god, bringing everything else into its service. However, the couple's other responsibilities just will not be fully subordinated to the marriage. If the husband devotes his energies to business, he is having an affair, instead of giving his all to the marriage. Marriages that have an idol-glow about them—trying to be everything—inevitably collapse.

Often both husband and wife choose different idols, the husband his business and the wife the family. The husband feels guilty when not working for the company, while the wife hates the business as a competitor to the family. The same problem arises when a non-Christian marries a Christian who confesses that only the kingdom of Jesus Christ is great enough to encompass everything in this life. If the believer takes on outside responsibility in an effort to serve the Lord, his unbelieving partner is apt to accuse him of being unfaithful to their marriage.

Only when the vision of Christ's kingdom guides both husband and wife will there be no difficulties in principle. Of course, Christians also have their problems trying to balance all their kingdom responsibilities. However, those tensions are minor compared to the inherent structural difficulties which beset a couple guided by an unbiblical vision.

When husband and wife confess that their marriage is only one part of the kingdom, neither accuses the other of infidelity if he spends time on other responsibilities. The wife will not look at the business as a competitor, nor will the husband look at the wife's career as a threat. Their bond of troth will deepen as their marriage finds its limited but essential place in their lives. In this way both will be better prepared to take up all of their tasks in the rooms of God's creation.

If marriage is not an idol, we don't have to demand that it satisfy all our needs. In fact, the man or woman who invests everything in his marriage simply overburdens the relationship and invites problems. Only when marriage takes its place as one relation among several others will it be able to grow and prosper. Christians need to apply Christ's law of the kingdom to marriage: "But seek first his kingdom and his righteousness, and all these things shall be yours as well" (Matt. 6:33).

Jesus Christ did not urge us to seek God's kingdom and ignore marriage as if it would take care of itself. Neither did he mean we should marry almost anyone who confesses Christ, as some seem to believe. Two Christians may agree on the basic vision of life, but they must also be able to work out their vision together in the concrete details of marriage. They need to enjoy each other's company, to have common interests, and to share a burgeoning troth. Otherwise, their common vision will remain lip-service without any meaningful function in their marriage.

Indeed, to seek the kingdom of God in marriage means that a man and a woman do everything in their power to explore and build up their relationship. If they work within the overarching perspective of the kingdom, God promises his blessing and the joys of a real marriage.

Marriage without Christ

If Jesus Christ is the ground of a healthy, satisfying marriage, what kind of marriage can develop between two people who do not confess Christ? The question is common but nearly always left unanswered. Usually commentators ignore the critical distinction between the all-motivating, all-encompassing love of God and one of the ways of loving God which we have called keeping troth. When the same word is used for both kinds of love, we encounter real problems. Can we really say that a man outside of Christ loves his wife? Is his love simply fake? Historically, men have tried to solve the problem by distinguishing between the self-giving character of agapic love and the selfish, physical love of eros. But can we honestly say that only Christians can really love their wives in a selfless agapic fashion? Part of the confusion arises because the agape-eros distinction is false. Eventually, it would lead us to conclude that loving God is not very important if marriages between non-Christians are as real as those between Christians. There must be another explanation.

Two traditions developed within the Christian church as men tried to resolve this problem. The more conservative often said that outside of Christ, husbands and wives do not and *cannot* really love each other. They believed that love in non-Christian marriages was superficial at best and mere pretense at worst. On the other hand, the more liberal saw many solid non-Christian marriages and many jittery Christian marriages. As a result, they minimized the love of God, sometimes by maintaining that non-Christians shared in it or at other times by singing the praise of human love and relegating the love of God to the higher, spiritual realms of church and grace. In their view a unique love of God had nothing to do with marriage, if it had any importance at all.

Both traditions are still alive. While some suggest that a mutual love of God is really the only important condition for marriage, others are concerned primarily with the physical and psychic dimensions of mar-

61

riage. Both views cause immense harm. For instance, a couple may experience difficulties and begin to doubt their faith. Since they feel reluctant to admit difficulties, they never ask for help for fear that others will question their commitment to Christ. At the same time, other couples lack meaning and unity in their relation, yet they never realize that it has anything to do with the love of God and his kingdom.

If both Christians and non-Christians run into problems, what difference can there be between the two kinds of marriage? All people—Christian or not—are called to meet God's structural norm of troth. However, men are also called to love as the directional motive force that leads and unfolds all their activities.

Any couple that marries obeys the call to troth to some degree. Without troth there would simply be no marriage. Since non-Christians also live under the structuring Word for marriage, they can really pledge troth and honestly love each other. In this sense they give honor to Christ and bow before his Word in spite of themselves. In fact, their marriage is a continual call to them from the Lord to turn to him. However, since they do not acknowledge in their hearts that the Lord is the giver and redeemer of life, they must live with a basic uncertainty, disunity, and distortion in their lives. Without the love of God in their hearts, the seed of distortion is in their marriage.

Adultery

Unfortunately, marriages can be broken in as many ways as they can be built. Husbands and wives can have affairs or squander their money. They might establish separate lives and merely sleep and eat under the same roof, or they might not stick by each other in joy and in sorrow. They might cut each other off and begin keeping secrets. Every couple can find countless ways to break their marriage. If they do not grow together in troth, their relation will stagnate and become boring. Boredom (coupled with the disappointments it brings) is the number one cause of physical infidelity.[2]

Adultery covers *all the ways* in which infidelity can take place in a marriage. It has no justification because continual adultery finally destroys a marriage and brings about its total, prolonged breakdown.

"You shall not commit adultery" is an Old Testament way of restating the Word for marriage. It is not a prohibition aimed at holding down man's evil sexual lusts, but a positive protection for full troth fulfillment. The seventh commandment or Word simply tells man that only in troth and fidelity can marriage be a blessing. Today it should perhaps read: "Keep the troth in marriage," or even, "Have fun in marriage." The Scriptures warn man against adultery because it breaks troth, destroys mutual freedom, and makes people unhappy. The Word is a cryptic warning protecting marriage. Since marriage does not break as fast as a crystal glass, people flirt with the idea that fidelity is not really affected by an indiscretion here and there. However, the Word reminds us to take care. The commandment is much like the "No Swimming" sign planted in front of a dangerous pond. The sign erectors are not killjoys who want to deprive sweaty children of some pleasant relief on a hot summer day. The signs go up because someone cares enough about life to try to prevent drowning. So it is with the seventh Word.

When God forbids adultery, he calls man to more than physical fidelity. Marriage is a total troth communion, which can be broken by any kind of infidelity, not just physical, as we have traditionally too often assumed.

A man and a woman may be unfaithful to each other in many different ways but not every infidelity must necessarily break up their marriage. Although Christ said that he who looks lustfully at a woman has already committed adultery with her in his heart (Matt. 5:28), he did not say that physical infidelity must lead inevitably to divorce. Husbands and wives must always be ready to forgive, for as it takes two to be faithful, it also takes two to be unfaithful. An innocent party seldom exists. Every kind of infidelity is an obstacle to be overcome if marriage is to grow. Infidelities ought to be occasions in which partners change their ways, forgive, and make up. The mutual pledge of troth demands such readiness and willingness to forgive.

Counseling

Everything possible must be done to heal a floundering marriage. A couple ought to seek help at the first sign of serious difficulties. Outside parties should see that counseling takes place in an aura of openness, concern, and understanding. All of us—friends, relatives, fellow Christians—could take our calling to be hands and feet to each other more seriously. If we show genuine concern for the welfare of others, we create a climate conducive to healing, a climate in which help, compassion, and even admonition can be more freely offered and more freely received. Creating this climate of service and concern is crucial if we are to resolve marriage problems before they become serious breaks. A couple ought to seek help at the first sign of serious difficulties rather than bungling along, as so often happens, until the marriage is in an advanced stage of disrepair.

Many couples whose marriages today end in the divorce courts could reestablish a healthy relationship with proper understanding and loving care. More couples need such care than we realize because vast numbers of men and women are abysmally ignorant of what marriage is at heart really all about. Misinformation and inadequate preparation for marriage go hand in hand to undermine a couple's relationship. Often in such cases the problem is not that the man and woman lack troth entirely, but that their troth has remained underdeveloped with the result that the marriage has gotten hung up at various points. With patience and guided homework such couples can begin to explore the causes of their breakdown, and they can discover new ways to foster and strengthen troth. They are able to gain real insight into themselves and their relationship. On the other hand, couples have much less chance for healing when they not only lack troth but are completely indifferent or are openly hostile to each other. Whatever the nature of the breakdown, the seriousness of the couple's situation cannot be ignored: to fail in marriage is to fail in one of the central relations in life.

Marriage counselors have a high calling: restoring troth and healing marriage. Their ability to help troubled couples depends on the attitude and the commitment with which they seek to reach this goal. Counselors must put themselves on the line and commit themselves to see the couple through their difficulties. Without such commitment the mutual trust is stifled before good things can happen. If the counselor (or counselors—often a team approach is ideal in marriage counseling) meets the problems head-on and listens empathetically, the husband and wife gather courage to explore situations they could not previously face, much less handle. The couple begins to disentangle the jumbled situation which threatens or already overwhelms them. This is in itself great progress: the couple learns to see that their marriage is more than the tangled areas which weigh them down at present, and they begin to see that tension in one area need not mean the marriage is doomed. They focus on the facet of their relationship which is especially troubled and which is slowly poisoning the marriage as a whole.

On the other hand, if the husband and wife begin to feel that the counselor is not pushing through to the heart of their problem (or might even be deliberately avoiding it), they easily conclude that their situation must be extremely critical—even too critical for the counselor. This leads them to hold back, making the whole counseling relationship a fruitless exercise.

Marriage Breakup

However, the breach between husband and wife sometimes refuses to be healed in spite of all efforts to restore the relationship. The bond of troth no longer exists between them. The state of total, prolonged breakdown has resulted in the death of the marriage. What ought to be —marriage troth—is not; what is—a dead marriage—ought not to be.

Once the marriage is dead, the family, friends, church, and state only acknowledge this sad fact. Just as the state legally recognizes the birth of a marriage by issuing a marriage license, it issues a writ of divorce as

65

the legal recognition that the marriage has died. The church, too, must acknowledge the fact even as it continues to minister to the persons concerned. If the church refuses to recognize the death of a marriage, it multiplies the sin by hypocritically maintaining an "empty shell" as a marriage. In such a case the church condemns two separated people to years of loneliness, years that are void of the joy and intimacy of a partner in troth. The church may even make a new and healthy troth relationship impossible by threatening the man and woman with excommunication if they remarry.

People suffering the pathos of divorce require intensive pastoral care, but formal ecclesiastical discipline should not begin automatically with the divorce decree. The couple should only be excluded from the Lord's table and subsequently excommunicated when they do not acknowledge and repent of the sins involved in the breakdown of their marriage.

The Gospel of Grace and Forgiveness

At this point it is important to note that the seriousness with which Christ treats adultery is only equal to his mercy for sinners, even adulterers. Christ's pardon of the woman caught in the act of adultery (John 8:1 ff.) is a graphic illustration. Recognizing divorce does not force us to waive the demand for complete faithfulness because we also acknowledge that such divorce involves sin requiring repentance.

Thus, it is difficult to understand the tendency in many Christian churches to excommunicate anyone involved in divorce, as if divorce were the cardinal sin which automatically made one an unbeliever. Apparently, a Christian may fail in every other area and be forgiven, but not in marriage.

Whatever refinements are employed to hide its basic thrust, this attitude is hostile to the Scriptures. To deny that repentance and forgiveness free a person from the sin of a broken marriage is to do violence to the gospel of forgiveness. No one is saved because his marriage is healthy, but neither is anyone lost because his marriage has failed. Only in God's grace can we have healthy marriages. Only his grace can save us from the wreckage of a broken marriage.

When we maintain that a writ of divorce is always wrong, we make an idol of marriage. When marriage is everything in a person's life, it is an idol condemned by Christ. Similarly, when maintaining a marriage with only a legal shell becomes everything, it is also an idol. When this sad policy is pursued rigorously, people are sometimes led to give up their commitment to the Lord. Their unmitigated marital disaster becomes the instrument by which their hearts turn bitterly from the Lord particularly as they are piously told in his name that they may not escape their dead marriage. Divorce, in such cases, should be read as the public admission and legal recognition that even with outside help the persons involved were not only unable to live in troth as husband and wife, but the failure to so live was threatening to destroy their personal integrity and endangering their commitment to the Lord.

A divorce does not make them non-Christians, who can become Christians once more when they "repent"—provided, of course, the divorce is not part of a total rejection of his ways. Rather the gospel of grace assures them, that in spite of serious sins in their lives, God hears their cry of repentance and offers forgiveness—in the same way he forgives his children of other offenses.

Biblical "Grounds" for Divorce?

Although divorces are to be recognized with regret, there are actually no biblical grounds for divorce. Some condemn divorce in general but maintain that an "innocent," abandoned partner has "biblical grounds for divorce." Often this so-called biblical divorce is an excuse for one of the parties to get out of the relationship. Even if one party is more innocent than the other, the relationship is still broken, a condition the Scriptures never condone.

Marriage is such an involved and intimate relationship that neither partner can claim to be "innocent," both morally and legally. Which husband or wife involved in marital difficulties can claim that he has not contributed to the breakdown in any way?

We often determine innocence or guilt by whether or not one partner has deserted the other or has had physical intercourse with a third party. But why does physical intercourse preoccupy us when we must determine guilt? What about all the other reasons which are at least equally involved in the breakdown? Doesn't this approach suggest that a couple must forgive every infidelity except physical? Furthermore, a partner who has not been physically unfaithful may still be considered "innocent" even if he refuses to forgive his repentant mate. Such "innocence" is certainly not biblical.

Where such limitations are common, one partner may be called "innocent" simply because he has not had physical intercourse with a third party. Yet both of them have been unfaithful in many other ways. A partner may bring about a marriage crisis by nagging, indifference, drinking, mistrust, or lying. However, he is likely to be exonerated because his "guilty" partner has been physically unfaithful as well.

Our preoccupation with physical infidelity has contributed to what is known as the "big lie"—arranged physical adultery to establish the state and the church's grounds for divorce. However, physical infidelity is more often a symptom of marital problems rather than the cause, more often resulting from rather than initiating breakdown. The real causes of marital breakdown will remain untouched as long as we focus only on physical infidelity.

Ironically the evangelical Christian church often naively considers adultery in strictly physical sexual terms, in much the same way that the society it condemns allows physical intercourse to dominate marriage rather than the troth commitment set forth in the biblical teaching on marriage. The implications of such a correspondence are sobering, particularly when we realize that many people outside the body of Christ are beginning to understand that there is much more to marriage than physical sexuality. In the Scriptures adultery covers every way of breaking troth. The unique structure of marriage means that infidelity of various kinds, if not checked, usually leads to physical adultery. Physical adultery in a special typical way characterizes marital infidelity in general. However we cannot define adultery in terms of the physical, for the basic meaning of even physical adultery is the breaking of troth.

Talk of "biblical grounds" for divorce is usually based on an interpretation of Matthew 19:9, "And I say to you: whoever divorces his wife, except for unchastity, and marries another, commits adultery," and a similar passage in Matthew 5:32. Mark 10:11 and Luke 16:18 are parallel passages without the clauses "except for unchastity" and "except on the ground of unchastity." The thrust of these four passages is unmistakable: marriage is of the Lord and is not to be broken. Christ is calling men and women to the norm of marital fidelity without exception. If a man has a wife, it is the height of infidelity to break the covenant with her and marry another woman. The clauses added in Matthew's account in no way diminish Christ's emphasis on the lifelong nature of marriage. But neither are they, I believe, to be read as giving grounds for divorce.

During Jesus' time Jewish divorce practice was lax and usually applied to men only. However, women were under strict laws. Under Roman pressure in A.D. 30 the death penalty for adulterous women was dropped.[3] It was replaced with a law forcing a husband to divorce his adulterous wife and forbidding the wife to marry her lover. Mandatory divorce was the penalty for extramarital intercourse for women. Jesus is concerned that men take the calling of unconditional fidelity as seriously as the women were forced to by law.

In contrast to the policy of double morality which originated in the Old Testament dispensation when only women were under the obligation to avoid all nonmarital intercourse, Christ affirms the equality of husband and wife before the norm of marriage. In fact this call to male fidelity strikes even the disciples so hard that they exclaim, "If such is the case of a man with his wife, it is not expedient to marry" (Matt. 19:10).

At the same time, Matthew's account, written especially for Jewish Christians, includes exceptive clauses in which Jesus assures Jewish husbands that he is aware that the law requires them to put away their unfaithful wives. In that case a husband is not guilty of forcing his wife to become an adulteress. She has already committed adultery.

This side reference to the possible necessity of divorce indicates that Christ recognizes divorce as a reality. However, these words, which appear to be directly related to the situation of that time, should not be used as grounds for divorce in every age. The conclusion drawn by Friederich Hauck and Sieffried Schulz in Kittel's *Theological Dictionary of the New Testament* is much more to the point: "The drift of the clauses, then, is not that the Christian husband, should his wife be unfaithful, is permitted to divorce her, but that if he is legally forced to do this he should not be open to criticism if by her conduct his wife has made the continuation of the marriage quite impossible."[4]

Apparently, Christ is not giving grounds for divorce at all. He recognizes the realities of the situation and condemns those who abuse the writ of divorce, not those who are forced by the law of the time to use it. His overriding concern is to teach the abiding character of marriage for all times and all places, and to have it apply equally to men and women.

After Divorce

The issue of divorce frequently raises questions about remarriage. Some declare remarriage is wrong on the basis of Christ's teachings in the passages we have just investigated and on Paul's words in 1 Corinthians 7. This position is difficult to maintain. Jesus emphatically condemns the putting away of a spouse for adulterous reasons; that is a clear case of adultery. However, the situation is different when the person is no longer married. Then, apparently, he or she is in principle free (though scarred, no doubt) to make new efforts to serve the Lord in marriage.

Paul's strictures in 1 Corinthians 7:10–16 are to be read as his efforts in times of great stress (v. 26) to regulate marital life with the minimum of upheaval in the light of the norm of lifelong fidelity.[5] To conclude that remarriage is always wrong from these passages is to misread Paul's specific measures as universal norms, rather than understanding them as ways of implementing universal norms. In general, since we know that God's grace is big enough to forgive divorce and the sins involved, there seems no good reason why the possibility of remarriage is not open to the Christian.

Remarriage does raise difficult matters. Divorced persons have experienced failure in one important part of their lives. They frequently have strong feelings of guilt, shame, and anger. Such people need help and understanding so that they can grow personally and avoid making the same mistakes again. Growth is essential, for unless divorced people acknowledge their part in the previous breakdown and show evidence that things will be different a second time, they have no reason to expect that a second marriage will be any better than the first. They should not remarry unless they genuinely try to understand what went wrong, why it went wrong, and why reconciliation attempts failed.

Christians often have the most difficult time in surviving a divorce. They rightly see marriage as a high and holy calling. Although they have failed and feel judged, they must realize that God's mercy is big enough to forgive the sins involved in marital failure too. Indeed, when they sincerely repent and ask for forgiveness, the possibility of new life in Jesus Christ is real, even in an area of previous failure.

Under the effects of sin, a marriage can often be a caricature of what it ought to be. Then God's Word for marriage comes to man in judgment. However, married couples who obey the norm of troth will experience great blessing. In Christ a marriage can continually deepen in meaning and take its place in the kingdom of God. In fact, Paul compares the intimacy, tenderness, and troth of the husband-wife relationship to the living relationship between Christ and the church (cf. Eph. 5:21–33).

NOTES

1. For most of this historical material I am indebted to E. Schillebeeckx, *Marriage: Secular Reality and Saving Mystery,* vol. 2, *Marriage in the History of the Church* (London: Sheed and Ward, 1965).

2. Morton M. Hunt's *The Affair* (New York: World Publishing Company, 1969) paints a graphic picture.

3. Gerhard Kittel, ed., *Theological Dictionary of the New Testament* (Grand Rapids: Wm. B. Eerdmans Publishing Company), vol. 4, p. 732, vol. 6, p. 592.

4. Gerhard Kittel, ed., *Theological Dictionary of the New Testament,* vol. 6, p. 592.

5. Paul opposes separation (v. 10) but at the same time recognizes that this may not always be avoidable (vv. 11, 15). And even when separation takes place, he attempts to reconcile by declaring that such a woman may not remarry, although here too he ends up under certain circumstances in allowing separation without forbidding remarriage. In fact he says that they are not "bound" (v. 15).

4

THE FAMILY: REST, ADVENTURE, AND GUIDANCE

Today is, in Toynbee's phrase, a "time of trouble." The disintegration rampant in our society touches everything, even the family. Even if the family members do not go their separate ways, more often than not the family is broken internally. Father, mother, and the children may eat and sleep at the same place, but that is about all they do at home. This family breakdown is all the more obvious when we consider the so-called youth problem. We are actually facing a family problem, not a youth problem. When a family lacks real ties and genuine parent-children relationships, the parents are just as involved as their children, if not more.

Some observers tell us that family breakdowns are inevitable because the Western nuclear family is inherently narcissistic, exploitative, and repressive. Therefore, some see family breakups as a sign that Americans are struggling to shake off a destructive system and to enter a new era of meaningful and voluntary relations. Before we can evaluate such a critique, we need to ask a few basic questions. Why did God give mankind the family structure? How did he intend that it be used? Just how does a genuine family come into being?

Family Planning

Although marriage and family are clearly two distinct relationships, they are usually intertwined. Nowhere does the interlocking character of marriage and the family surface as concretely as in the matter of family planning. Together husband and wife must decide whether they wish to begin a family. Their choice is most important and its consequences far-reaching.

If we see that the question of family planning occurs within the context of a marriage, we avoid the common error of dealing with it as an abstraction. Since we can only judge whether birth control is morally right or morally wrong within the confines of an individual marriage, we cannot say that birth control, in itself, is always right or always wrong. Within the marriage family planning will always be a part of mankind's task to have dominion. Simply being married forces a couple to plan whether or not they will have children. The basic question they must ask is whether or not the control they exercise serves the coming of Christ's kingdom. An abstract yes or no is not acceptable because every couple's situation is different. If a couple decides not to have children for selfish reasons, birth control is wrong. Another couple may be justified in foregoing children for the sake of the kingdom, perhaps to serve as missionaries in tribal lands where children cannot be adequately cared for. The morality of their decision depends on ethical, economic, psychic, physical, and other considerations. Just as some people are eunuchs for the kingdom (Matt. 19:12), some couples may go childless for the kingdom. Again as in the case of eunuchs, such couples are more often the exception than the rule.

Neither can there be a set rule as to the number of children a family should have. The makeup of each family differs just as family circumstances range all the way from urban ghettos to sprawling ranches, from families on welfare to affluent suburbanites. Even more important, parents differ greatly in their ability to cope with the stresses of raising a family. Moreover, children today require much personal and individual attention to prepare them to cope with our complex society. Perhaps a family is too large when everything necessarily gravitates around the children's needs and too small when everything gravitates around the parents' needs. Probably few parents and few children can really adequately cope when there are six or more children. At the same time, one-child families appear to be less than desirable.

The method of birth control a couple uses in family planning is a secondary matter. It should be effective, safe, and as unobtrusive as possible. Ordinarily, it will be so-called artificial means, though the word *artificial* prejudices the case. Artificial means of birth control are no more artificial than any other technique invented by man. The point is that the means we use should be human means of birth control; yet the so-called natural means of birth control are actually rather inhuman and unnatural for man. To force a woman to conceive "naturally" according to biophysical patterns is to treat her as an animal. In contrast to the animals, God made man to choose whether to be a parent or not. To prohibit that free choice is dehumanizing. When a couple moves toward intercourse as an expression or deepening of troth, it is unnatural for them to abstain out of fear of pregnancy. This fear is particularly intense on the part of the many women who know they will be saddled with the full care of the child. In the long run it is immoral and undermines the marriage itself; the pathetic testimony of hyperfertile and "frigid" wives suggests the destruction such "natural" means can bring. Similarly, the rhythm method turns intercourse into a mechanical release of "sexual drive" to take place only during the so-called safe period rather than at the appropriate times husband and wife themselves choose. With both the abstention and the rhythm methods the couple loses the spontaneity that is essential to intercourse if it is to strenghten their troth. In general each couple must mutually decide for themselves what form of birth control best serves their situation. To make no decision in the effort to be "natural" could produce too large a family or a marriage in which intercourse becomes an occasional skirmish between a "desperate" husband and a fearful wife.

Adoption

Today, because of the more highly developed means of birth control, the decision to have or not to have children is more complex. The other

side of the birth control coin is adoption. Couples who cannot obtain a family through the normal way of reproduction can obtain a child through adoption. This possibility too is a real blessing of the Lord. Parents can have children even if they cannot bear them, and parents can control conception even if they can have children.

Artificial Insemination

For some couples the problem is not birth control but infertility. Many choose to adopt children, while a few select artificial insemination. According to the troth norm of marriage, artificial insemination would appear to be permissible only when the donor is the husband (A.I.H.). Artificial insemination from an anonymous donor (A.I.D.) breaks the mutuality of marriage on the biotic level, straining and even violating the fellowship of marriage on all other levels. When a wife achieves motherhood on the biotic level but the husband does not achieve a biotic fatherhood, the solidarity of their marriage is broken down. Marriage means sharing everything. If the husband is impotent or the wife infertile, both should mutually bear the burden. Although together they may be biologically childless, they can have children by adoption. And since father and mother are basically troth figures, they are parents in the fullest sense of the word when they are faithful in their loving care and concern for the children.

Abortion

Although the matter cannot be examined in detail, the question of abortion cannot be avoided.[1] In some circles abortion is advocated as another form of family planning. On the contrary, abortion is not the planning of a family or the prevention of conception, but the aborting of a potential family member.

Much of the discussion centers around whether or not the fetus is human and when it becomes human. Although the issue is important,

the answers are not clear-cut. Even if people agree on whether or not the fetus is human, they often disagree on whether or not abortion is legitimate. The confusion is not surprising. Apparently the orgánism possesses all the potentialities for humanity in its genes and in this sense is human from the moment of conception (which itself is more of a process than a single, indisputable moment in time). And certainly the fetus has a well-defined human shape, even at two months. Yet, no child reckons his birthday from his moment of conception. Everyone recognizes that there is a significant difference between a fetus and a newly born child. A fetus exists in a twilight zone: it is becoming, already-human, and not yet human.

Beyond doubt, life—including potential human life—is to be preserved rather than destroyed. An emphasis on the value of the fetal life may be necessary and just, but it cannot resolve all the difficulties in this issue. Since nearly everyone agrees that maternal life is also valuable, we usually allow abortions if the mother's life is at stake. Many wonder if cases of rape, incest, and even extreme socioeconomic problems might not justify an abortion.

We can sort out some of the problems if we look at distressed pregnancies in context. Children are born into families as a result of the troth-communion of husband and wife, sealed in physical intercourse. All who engage in such intercourse promise implicitly to take care of the fruit of their labor. Willingness to engage in physical intercourse includes the mutual promise of troth to bear the responsibility of the act. By that criterion most abortions are simply ruled out as immoral. Pregnancies resulting from affairs are not exceptions since affairs are voluntary matters. At the same time, the mutual-troth character of intercourse destroys the argument that the woman has control of her own body and that therefore abortion is her sole concern. Of course a woman as an individual controls her own body. The point is that both the man and the woman voluntarily give up their bodies to their mates when they have sexual intercourse. The resulting pregnancy is their mutual responsibility.

77

Under the guidance of the norm of troth we are also able to see our way through the small number of exceptional or abnormal cases. Abortion is justified when unforeseen circumstances endanger the mother's life. The husband must still honor his commitment to nourish and protect his wife even though both have promised to accept the responsibilities of intercourse. Likewise, due to its involuntary nature, in cases of rape (including involuntary incest) abortion would be permissible. If the parents did not know of the danger beforehand, abortion is also a possibility when a doctor discovers that the fetus will probably be extremely deformed or an imbecile. Hopefully, genetic counseling will be more widely available in the future to help parents make wise decisions with a minimum of risk.

The norm of troth and its responsibilities are so important that our emphasis should be on preventing the situation that leads people to ask for abortion, rather than just preventing women from destroying unwanted life. We should do everything to make sure life is wanted and planned in troth, for then it will be loved.

Mutuality in troth is the crux of the matter. "In troth" because where troth is lacking in name-only marriages, couples should not imagine that having children will solve the problems. "Mutuality" in order that husbands realize that they have no right to force pregnancy upon their wives and in order that wives realize they have no right to beg off intercourse and family simply to get even with their husbands.

The Family Itself

The family is a gift of the Lord to mankind, a "room" in the creation for man's benefit. God did not leave man alone in an uncharted, unstructured world; rather, he so structured the world by his creative Word that man could know how to live. As a human community the family is structurally anchored in the law-order of God and takes its place as one of the central "rooms" in the creation.

Man comes to life in the family; he learns to love in the family. The

78

family is his nursery, his first school; it is his initial world and his launching pad into the big outdoors. As he participates in the family, he experiences the diversity of life without having to bear full responsibility for all that happens. The family is his place of joy and sadness; it is the place where he learns to take and bear responsibility. In the family he learns the meaning of keeping his word. In the family he learns to express his feelings and to know himself; he finds his identity; he experiences intimacy. Without the family the young child stands unprotected against the world. Without a family a child is alone, forced to live before he has even learned how. Nothing is more tragic than children worn out by life just when life should be opening up its riches.

Troth Is the Key

The family ought to be a community of troth between parents and children based on the instinctual biotic drive for motherhood and fatherhood and on the subsequent blood ties. Again, the key word here is *troth*, that is loyalty, trust, fidelity, devotion, and reliability. Troth is a pledged vow; it is the central norm or standard to be worked out in the family. In the measure that troth develops, a family prospers: loyal, trustworthy parents make for loyal, trustworthy children and vice versa. Likewise, unfaithful children and unfaithful parents belong together. Family relations are reciprocal and interdependent in nature. The family is a call to intimacy.

The fact that children are born into a family (or are adopted into it) does not in itself make a family. The arrival of children is only the basis upon which a family must be built. Blood ties provide the foundation for the family unit—but that is all. In contrast to animals, man's biopsychic structures require unfolding under the leading of other human dimensions. Even eating is not simply a biophysical matter for man. The mastication and digestion of food is only one part—albeit essential—of the family dinner, the business luncheon, the alumni banquet, state dinner, and the midnight snack. In any case blood ties by themselves are not enough to ensure troth in the family, for fathers and mothers can turn on their children. Unless father and mother exercise troth in nurturing their children, they are not really fathers and mothers in the basic sense. If troth is exercised, even if the children are adopted, the parenthood is true. Sometimes a child knows and feels that his real parent is someone other than his "natural" parent.

Becoming a parent is not the trick; it is being a parent. A family must work at developing, strengthening, and conserving the bond of troth between its members. Only then is there a real family. All family activities—balancing the budget, attending worship services, skating, and just plain living—are to take place under the norm of troth. Father, mother, and child are called to intimacy. They are devoted to each other, they help each other, and they pledge their love to each other. In this kind of unity they are a family.

Nurture

In the intimacy of the family, parents must lead, educate, steer, guide, and nurture their children so that they come to see the norms that hold for life and so that they will be able to bear the responsibility of living according to these norms. Although others may point their children to other standards, Christian parents must help their children see the Lord's norms for life so that they can wholeheartedly serve him. Out of love the parents must guide their children so carefully that they will gradually come to accept responsibility for their own lives. Their goal is to prepare their children to live responsible, useful lives as the Lord's representatives.

Family Forms in History

Throughout history the basic structure God gave for the family has remained unchanged, yet the family has assumed remarkably different forms. For example, today's family is very different from the families of the Old and New Testament eras, the Middle Ages, or even the 1800s. The form the family takes on—the decoration of the family room of the creation—can even change from generation to generation and from society to society without destroying the family structure. Abraham was not only husband and father, he was employer, king, head of the army, high priest, educator, and so on. In earlier times the family was a diversified unit responsible to produce and consume goods, lead the worship, carry out political and educational duties, and provide the members with emotional security, protection, and practice in getting along with others.

Over the centuries the family has given up most of these tasks, leaving them to the confessional, economic, social, political, and educational communities that developed. Today the family must stand on its own two feet: it either survives as a family, or it dissolves altogether. Most of the needs men used to satisfy at home can now be met outside. The external props that often held families together—economic, social, educational, religious, or whatever—are largely gone; the family must do it on its own. In the days before foster homes, youth hostels, and social services, children who didn't particularly like their families usually stayed at home because they needed a place to sleep and someone to prepare dinner. These "needs" often kept the family together even without a bond of trust.

Today, increasing numbers of young people are leaving home prematurely. They find it easy to get around, and independence is so valued that adults no longer expect them to stay at home until they marry. The broken family, hiding behind economic interests, physical necessities, or social considerations, would find little reason to stay together today. With greater prosperity and a widespread fear of repression, families are less likely to live together at any cost. In danger or bad times, however, the family tends to stay together. This loss of external supports for the family is causing problems for many sociologists who overlook the troth structure of the family and declare that the nuclear family has four essential functions: socialization, economic cooperation, reproduction, and sexual relations.[2] If those actually are the essential functions of the family, its final breakdown is almost certain.

Family Survival

To be strong today the family must depend upon the quality of the troth or fidelity in its family relations. The family does not stand or fall today as a church, or as a business, but as a family. As never before, the family can concentrate on its own business rather than taking care of basically nonfamily matters.

We need not grieve over the family's loss of its nonessential functions. Actually, we ought to be encouraged because now our families are free to get on with their own concerns. When the family served such a wide range of interests (often in jack-of-all-trades-and-master-of-none style), the true nature of the family as a community of bonded troth did not take on visible form.

At the same time, we must admit that external duties and activities often threaten the modern family's freedom to be a family. If father is not working, he is out golfing. If mother is not serving as a taxi for the children, she is at the church or a volunteer group. Johnny has his hockey and guitar, and Janny her baseball and ballet. If family members are always on the run, family life is bound to suffer.

The solution to this problem, however, is not to cut off all outside contacts in an attempt to make the family self-sufficient once again. Rather, we need to seek a pattern of life which gives the family its due as a unique place of troth instead of a competitor of peer, church, or business groups. For when the family is a place of rest, joy, and authenticity, family members will experience its uniqueness and increasingly desire the ease and assurance of its style. Instead of slowly sliding into complete breakdown, the family grows stronger as both outside pursuits and intimate family experiences take their indispensable and interlocking places. The family begins to serve as a power-center, a place where the family members are built up and in turn build each other up.

In such a family each member—father, mother, child—can meet his unique needs, follow his own interests, and develop his peculiar talents. Mothers and fathers can let their own form of family living emerge within a home set up for the family's unique way of life. Today's family has countless possibilities for God-glorifying family life, but it also has possibilities for dishonoring God in family life. Popular writers identify all sorts of obstacles to healthy family life—money problems, crowded quarters, unfulfilled mothers, infidelity, the so-called generation gap. However, a family can face these problems if its members follow the norm of troth in living with each other. Without the intimacy of that commitment and without the external supports of the past, it is no wonder that families break down all around us. Moreover, as developing and fostering troth is no easy matter—even when we are aware of its importance—the modern family is extremely fragile.

Home Is Rest

Establishing families as troth communities is no easy matter. We are helped in this situation to think of the family as a place of rest, adventure, and guidance. The family is first of all a place of rest. The family home is a place of troth, security, and peace, where a child can come to himself and can feel safe—no matter what. He knows that he will always be accepted, even if he does poorly in school, even if he can't do arithmetic and his father wants him to take over the family business, even if he does not want to be a farmer and his father has the best farm in the country. He can count on his parents, and they can count on him. He does not have to worry about being the best at everything or about proving himself. He knows that his parents will love him even if he does not meet their expectations.

The child who is fully accepted at home can grow and discover his own identity without looking for meaning in tests of physical daring or in sexual attractiveness. Consequently, he develops a certain self-confidence and aplomb in doing some things well. Nothing is more important for a child than his parents' acceptance, and there is nothing that he senses sooner than their rejection. He needs to know that his parents will stand by him always. They may not approve, but they will understand. Such unconditional acceptance is the birthright of every child; without it family troth cannot develop as it should.

Regrettably, many modern families make love conditional. The child hears his parents' message: "If you fulfill this goal or accomplish that purpose, you will be wanted and loved." He feels the constant pressure to succeed, to match the accomplishments of a petted high-achiever. Meanwhile he becomes miserable and insecure.

Even permissive parents attach strings to their love; if they do all they can for their children, they naturally expect that their children will indulge their every whim in return. Often the child becomes emotionally insecure because he is overwhelmed with the obligation to fulfill his parents' wishes. Such conditional love is both destructive and contrary to the norm of troth for the family.

Most of us are guilty of conditional love at one time or another. Mother says, "If you don't eat Wheaties, you won't grow strong—and mom won't love you." Father chimes in, "If you don't drink milk, you won't grow strong—and dad won't love you." Although not always spoken, such bargains are outright emotional blackmail. The child is caught. He wants his parents' love—but not with strings attached. So he eats—sometimes, and sometimes he rebels.

Once the child begins the uncertain task of trying to earn his parents' love, he loses the freedom and trust he needs to learn to know himself. He becomes anxious and uncertain of his own worth. He begins to read any critique from his parents as confirmation of the rejection he fears.

In families where intimacy and troth are guaranteed, a child develops roots and matures as a person. He learns to accept critique as constructive rather than a personal attack. No one needs masks in such a home because parents and children are authentic, free to be themselves and express their real feelings and opinions. The rest of the family may not always approve of these feelings and opinions, but they always respect them. Together the family will work through their differences and express their joy and sorrow. Troth enables people to live freely, authentically, joyfully before the Lord. Children don't have to struggle for their parents' attention. Their parents tell them openly, warmly about life, about sex and health, about the meaning of troth, about whatever children want to know. Since they can disagree without breaking their trust, the family can discuss anything, knowing that they can count on each other's help, encouragement, and understanding.

To foster the kind of family troth that makes for healthy nurture, the parents must provide consistency and stability. Children can learn to count on their parents' word if they are treated consistently. Hasty or idle threats which parents should not or cannot carry out only leave them open to a child's understandable attempts to wear his parents down through continual badgering. If parents have not kept their word in the past, the child knows it only takes time. A parent who usually resists a little girl's pleas for money or cookies sometimes gives in if the child will go outside and leave him alone. Though the child may enjoy the cookies, she soon understands that the parent is really trying to get rid of her. That is deeply unsettling. At the same time, she will put her new knowledge to good use to get what she desires, even if she has to pit her mother and father against each other.

Home Is Adventure

The first priceless gift parents can give their children is roots. The second is wings. Safe in the security of his home, the child gains confidence and is encouraged to look to the world beyond the family. Guided by his parents the child tries different activities and learns what he does well and what he does badly. He opens up to the world and discovers that the family is not closed off in itself, but is one part of the kingdom of God. Family projects, everyday adventures, and times of deep family sharing kindle his spontaneity, creativity, and individuality. Parents can learn to take advantage of these spontaneous experiences so that every member of the family finds them deeply satisfying and rewarding. It is first of all the quality and not the quantity of the time spent with children that counts. As long as children feel unpressured and confident in their parents, they will be eager to learn, to take up projects, and to go on adventures of their own.

Home Is Guidance

While the home is a place of troth and adventure, it is also a place of guidance. In his adventurous spirit the child learns from his parents that there are right and wrong ways to live. His parents provide guidelines that will help him live better just as the white lines on the highway help drivers. From time to time when the child disregards his parents' guidelines, he must be punished. Disobedience endangers lives and cannot go unchecked. If parents are not concerned about correcting their children, the children soon sense that the parents do not really care what they do. On the other hand, discipline builds the family even though the child may put up a fuss. The child knows his parents care about the way he walks in life. He also knows that his parents stick by their word.

The Scriptures are emphatic about parents' need to guide their children in the right way. "He who spares the rod hates his son, but he who loves him is diligent to discipline him" (Prov. 13:24). "Discipline your son while there is hope; do not set your heart on his destruction" (Prov. 19:18). Such nurture gives delight and peace of mind to those who give it (Prov. 29:17) and life to those who receive it (Prov. 4:13). The Scriptures are not saying that every parent must physically beat his child with a stick. In terse, urgent tones they are urging parents to understand their awesome responsibility. Nothing may be left undone or untried; everything possible must be done to nurture children in the fear of the Lord. Nurture is a life-and-death matter.

Guidance in the home is not just rule upon rule, ordinance upon ordinance. Instead, the parents give positive guidance to their youngsters because they know their job is to train them to take responsibility. In giving guidance parents ought to resist the tendency to be hasty and judgmental. The parent who yells thief every time one of the children takes a cookie without permission is asking for trouble. The child may think that his mother really thinks he is a thief. And if he is a thief, of course he is guilty. Then it is but a short step for such a child to begin to live up to his name. The same thing happens to the child who is always berated for being messy, or late, or deceitful, or withdrawn. He takes on the role because that is what his parents think of him anyway.

This does not mean that punishment and correction are out of order. The point is that when parents correct their children—whether positively or negatively—they need to be sympathetic and understanding. And in their zeal to help their children they must not exaggerate the seriousness of the situation. Neither should they reject the child or correct him to vent their frustration. Parents especially need to resist the temptation to judge before they know the reasons for the child's behavior. A child who talks back is not necessarily challenging parental authority. The child is telling the parent something; neither a severe reprimand nor indifference will help him. In all likelihood his obstinancy is a cry for understanding and help. By misbehaving or challenging his parents he takes out his frustration on a person very close to him. If this person misreads his "disobedience" and rejects him, to whom can he now turn?

Unhealthy Family Form I: Father Knows Best

If troth in the family is not as it ought to be, the parents will not be able to nurture their children and prepare them to face life's challenges. The children will not come to know themselves, to bear responsibility, or even gain confidence in working out the meaning of their lives. Nearly everyone senses the seriousness of the problem, but no one offers real solutions. No wonder. The problem is so much bigger than an individual family or a group of families that parts of it are far beyond their control. In fact, two ways of nurturing our children in Western society further undermine the development of family troth; yet they are common and accepted.

Unconsciously parents generally bring up their children either as they were brought up or as their neighbors are bringing up their children. Therefore their nurturing usually becomes either *authoritarian* or *permissive*. However, instead of allowing family intimacy to unfold and develop as it should, both views lead to family breakdown.

Authoritarian families usually center around the parents, who see authority as an end in itself. Their children must obey—exactly as the parents have prescribed. They consider even small infractions of the house rules to be a clear challenge to their authority. Parents demand unquestioned obedience from their children; after all, the parents have absolute authority. The climate at home is rigid, something like a military barracks. Johnny must always be on his best behavior—or else. The father knows what is best for his family; he is always right—even before he knows Johnny's side of the story. Being the absolute authority, he does not even need to know his side.

Quite often Christian homes are even worse than their humanistic counterparts because the parents claim that God is on father's side. Gradually the children learn to think of God as a bigger version of father, stricter, less flexible, less merciful, completely self-serving.

In such homes Johnny learns to do as he is expected to do. If he "obeys," he will be left alone even if he only goes through the motions. He never really learns to obey from his heart because he wants to; he never learns to decide responsibly that a certain course of action is right or wrong. That is why the children in authoritarian homes often go wild when father and mother are no longer watching. Without father and mother they are either lost in new situations (in which case they look for someone else to issue orders), or they cavort like young colts let out to pasture for the first time.

Unhealthy Family Form II: The Fun-Family

Authoritarian families are not as common as they once were. In fact, in North America the majority of homes practice the permissive type of nurture, even among Christians. Children can do more or less as they please because everything at home centers around them and their desires. This is the permissive society, the fun-morality syndrome. Parents are merely older friends of their children. Since they have more experience in living, it usually pays off to listen to them. On the one hand the child is pampered; on the other hand he is his parents' "plaything." Instead of providing a climate which leads the children to commit themselves responsibly to the Lord and to obey his Word, the parents place the children themselves and their needs in the center of attention. Even if they pay lip-service to Almighty God, family life centers around their possessions and good times.

If Peter can do as he pleases in the family, he will want to do the same in all other relationships. Instead of becoming independent, Peter grows into adulthood completely dependent on his parents who indulge his every wish. Parents who do everything for their children naturally expect their children to appreciate their sacrifices and carry out their wishes. But a child often catches on to how much he "owes" his parents. Instead of feeling secure in the evidence of his parents' love, he begins to fear losing it if he does not fulfill their demands.

In permissive homes the children begin life by doing as they please; yet they feel the need for guidance and direction. If the parents do not set the norms they are to obey clearly before them, the children use their parents' personal wishes as the guidelines. What looks like an unrepressed family actually turns out to be authoritarian.

The authoritarian and permissive types of families are not only each other's opposites, they are also each other's complements. In our efforts to avoid the repression and restrictiveness of authoritarianism, we sometimes reject all authority and choose permissiveness instead. Permissiveness, in turn, leads to frustration which leads to a new form of authoritarianism. Children cannot grow up as they ought if they are continually told what to do and how to do it and if they are never encouraged to bear responsibility. Neither can they grow up as they ought if they are left to their own devices.

Basically, the crisis of authority today is the clash between these two attitudes. Authority-figures want to hold the line; many others are just as intent on doing away with all authority relations. Like a Ping-Pong ball, Western society bounces from one extreme to the other.

In the middle of all this stand the real victims—our children. The lack of genuine nurture in the family is one of the major causes of emotionally disturbed children. Widespread drug use is also clearly connected with the teenager's search for meaning he did not find at home. Any social worker, pastor, or probation officer can furnish innumerable examples of the sad results of either the authoritarian or permissive family.

Thus far we have assumed that families are either solidly authoritarian or permissive. Often, however, the father is the authority-figure and the mother is permissive, or the other way around. Here the child becomes a Ping-Pong ball, bounced back and forth until he cracks.

The current debate about the nature of discipline—authoritarian or permissive—will continue its pendulumlike swing without any real advance unless the discussion ranges deeper and wider. For it is especially on a deeper level that both attitudes fail. With the authoritarian emphasis on the need for the "big stick" and the permissive stress on "no stick," children have difficulty in experiencing the family as a we-situation of rest, adventure, and guidance. The troth character of the family which guarantees children their parents' unconditional acceptance, constant support, and deep understanding is fractured. Permissive families breed insecurity and undercut troth by leaving children alone, without guidance. Authoritarian families also leave their children on their own, except when they disobey the house rules of which their parents are guardians, and even then they feel more judged than understood. What children require most—living along in troth—is missing. Both ways are methods of avoiding intimacy.

The importance of this underlying, overarching, lived-in troth for the family cannot be overexaggerated. With intimacy in action families are basically on the right track whether or not they tend to be authoritarian or permissive. Without it families miss the boat regardless of how many or how few rules they have.

The answer to the authoritarian-permissive dilemma is not just carefully balancing the two family styles, but in a third alternative: a biblical view of the family and of family nurture. Since we have already described the troth intimacy of the family as a community of parents and children, we can move on and further explore what it means in terms of the parents' task to nurture and the child's task to mature.

The Parental Office

Human lives are so important that the Lord established the family and gave parents authority to help them in their awesome task. For their part the children are to submit themselves to this authority. The parents are duty-bound to lead the children to trust and follow the guidance; and both the leading and the following must be under the norm of familial troth. Parents' authority—qualified as it is by troth—elicits and awakens the children's trust. Parents have won the trust of their children when they can trust them to follow their leading. Children have won the trust of their parents when they are entrusted with the freedom to follow.

When the parents don't exercise their authority in love, the family is not living up to its norm. In fact, the parents abuse their office and disobey the Lord if they conceive of their authority as an end in itself, as if they can use their office for their own benefit. Parents have authority for the sake of the freedom of the children—and for no other reason. They must not in an authoritarian way lay down the law to suit themselves. The rules they establish are teaching tools to help the children respond properly. Parental authority is to be used for the welfare of the children and the family as a whole. It is not an excuse for a father or mother to introduce arbitrary rules to keep the children under control and quiet.

Parental authority meets the child's need for guidance, love, and help. It is intended to lead him, not to restrict him. As the child grows older the parents must more and more involve him in the family's decision making. He needs to go out on his own without his parents always sitting on top of him. If he acts responsibly, he gets more opportunities to develop on his own. In such ways a child's spontaneity, originality, and spirit are stimulated rather than killed.

When the child finally reaches maturity, his parents have finished their work; they are no longer needed as guides—at least most of the time. Although parents often feel badly at this point, they ought not to grieve. The fact that their child can leave the family home, able to stand on his own feet in God's grace, is the crowning touch of their labors. If the child has learned to walk in the fear of the Lord, the parents can rejoice at his blessing on their years of hard work. At this stage children are no longer subject to their parents' authority, but they continue to show respectful love for parents.

God gave man the family so that children could be helped to grow up. Mothers and fathers dishonor God when they try to keep their children young. Parents who keep their children dependent only frustrate them, sometimes making them emotional cripples for life. We may joke about the overprotective mom who smothers her children or about the absentee father who expresses his love in gifts, but many parents come dangerously close to the stereotypes. Children are not the property or playthings of their parents; they are "trusts" given to parents by the Lord.

Children are real people and from the beginning are to be respected as responsible beings before the Lord. Their lives are also responses to the Lord. Although it is the springtime of life, youth is a phase of life, and all human life is to be a response to the Lord. The parental task can be characterized in terms of responsibility. Parents are responsible to lead their children to take growing responsibility until they reach maturity in the family. Parents stand alongside their children, not over against them.

Honor Parents

According to the Scriptures, parents and children live under the promises and demands of the kingdom of God. Family life must be integrated, deepened, and enriched by the leading of belief. "Honor your father and your mother, that your days may be long in the land which the Lord your God gives you" (Exod. 20:12). The family is part of God's covenant to his people. Within that covenant his faithfulness to his people is from generation to generation. Honor of father and mother is the law of the kingdom. Or as Paul puts it: "Children, obey your parents in everything, for this pleases the Lord" (Col. 3:20). Why do children obey their parents? Because we are united in love in Christ. Our love for Christ shows up in the family room of the creation as honor, trust, and obedience to parents. Children must not forget this.

God desires the children to come to him by means of the parents. Thus, the Scriptures tell children to ask their parents about God and his mighty acts (Deut. 32:7; cf. also Exod. 12; 26; 13:14; Deut. 6:20; Josh. 4:6). In Deuteronomy God addresses the people. "And these words which I command you this day shall be upon your heart; and you shall teach them diligently unto your children, and shall talk of them when you sit in your house, and when you walk by the way, and when you lie down, and when you rise" (Deut. 6:6–7).

Parents are God's representatives in their families. It is up to them to bring the Word in the family and in turn to speak trustworthy words and to do true deeds. They are to live this way because children naturally look to their parents for guidance. A young boy accepts his father's word as truth because it is his father's word, and a young girl believes what her mother says because it is her mother speaking. Parents who betray that trust and deceive their children destroy the basis for a normal relationship, particularly for older children who have a right to ask for further explanations. When they live the truth, the children can obey their parents' word—trustingly, freely, willingly, and gladly. In this way parents are to lead them to accept the Word of the Lord. Bringing the Word to children is so important that the Scriptures frequently condemn disobedience of parents with heightened seriousness (cf. Prov. 30:17; 20:20; Deut. 27:16; Exod. 21:17, 15; Rom. 1:30; 2 Tim. 3:2).

The Lord tells children to honor their parents "that their days may be long and that it may be well with them in the land which the Lord will give." He tells parents to give their children the knowledge and wisdom necessary to live as God's children in God's land. No one can live in God's land without observing his rules and laws. Children are to ask their parents the whys, hows, whats, and wherefores. Parents are to answer.

When children allow themselves to be guided and instructed, they are honoring their fathers and mothers. In the Scriptures honor means willingness to learn from one's parents. It means trusting that one's parents are going the right way. Obedience to parents is not obedience period, obedience without a purpose. Children obey their parents because parents know the way of life for themselves and for their children.

Parental Responsibility

Being the kind of parent the Scriptures describe is dangerous, an extremely risky and terrifying responsibility. There are so many ways parents can lead their children astray or alienate them. One way is to guide them only in matters of clothes, good manners, and clean faces when they really need guidance in wisdom and foolishness, faith and unbelief. A child learns to walk, talk, care for his body, keep promises, handle money, appreciate art and music. He also learns to confess his faith in the Lord.

The parents' responsibility is so important that the Scriptures lay more emphasis on the sins and shortcomings of the parents than on those of their children. The fifth commandment—to honor father and mother—is two-sided: the children are to follow, but the parents must lead properly. This special attention to the parents begins already in the second commandment: "You shall not bow down to them or serve them; for I the Lord your God am a jealous God, visiting the iniquity of the fathers upon the children to the third and fourth generation of those who hate me" (Exod. 20:5). In the New Testament Paul instructs the children to obey and then warns, "Fathers, do not provoke your children to anger, but bring them up in the discipline and instruction of the Lord" (Eph. 6:4). "Fathers, do not provoke your children, lest they become discouraged" (Col. 3:21). The Heidelberg Catechism has caught the spirit here. Lord's Day 39 asks children to have patience with the shortcomings of their parents.

Now children in the Scriptures do resist their parents and the God of their parents, but in every case their parents started them on this path of disobedience. Cain's murder follows hard upon the fall of Adam and Eve (Gen. 3 and 4). Noah's drunkenness preceded Ham's indecency (Gen. 9:20–27). Lot's family problems started with his selfish choice (Gen. 13:5–13; 19:30–38). The rivalry between Jacob and Esau began with the foolish preferences of Isaac and Rebekah (Gen. 27). The scandal of Eli's sons is placed at Eli's door (1 Sam. 2:12–17, 22; 3:13). David's adultery leads to the rebellion of his sons (Ammon, 2 Sam. 13; Absalom, 2 Sam. 13–18; Adonijah, 1 Kings 1; 2 Sam. 11).

Jesus Christ reminded parents of the importance of leading children to God's Word in Matthew 18:5–7: "Whoever receives one such child in my name receives me; but whoever causes one of these little ones who believe in me to sin, it would be better for him to have a great millstone fastened round his neck and to be drowned in the depth of the sea."

Limited Authority

Since parents are under God's authority, their own is limited and conditional. Parents are to set the vision in which the family's living and learning is to take place. They are to give their children a framework for finding meaning in the specialized knowledge they gain later. But parents who lose the vision can lead on wrong paths; in that case, their rules lose their real meaning as guidelines or guideposts to the kingdom of heaven. In despair—because people perish for lack of vision (Prov. 29:18)—parents either see their rules as hitching posts, which children obey to achieve salvation, or they give up rules altogether.

When parents forget that their authority is for the freedom of their children, when they no longer see their task in the total context of God's kingdom, when they lack insight into the task at hand, they have nothing fundamental to say to their children. They have betrayed their parental office. They may be able to give advice and guidance on all kinds of matters, but without an integrating overview to give meaning to the details, their advice is haphazard and uneven. Without the insight of a vision of life parents cannot teach children proper priorities. Family life will drift aimlessly or it will stagnate.

Such parents can really no longer claim the obedience of their children because they have abused their office. They are unfaithful office bearers with a hollow authority which they artificially maintain at all costs or recklessly abdicate at high cost.

Abuse of Office

If parents abuse their office and become either authoritarian or permissive, they risk serious consequences. If they do not lead their children from a vision of the coming kingdom, they can no longer legitimately demand that their children adopt their way of life. Little children may not realize what is happening, but a young person who has been caught by the vision of the kingdom will probably realize that his life is being systematically misdirected. After much struggle, prayer, and discussion he may even have to abandon his parents' life-style. When a youngster is being led astray by his parents (and let's not hide the fact that this is also happening in the Christian church), he is being ruined for life. If God leads such a person to the way, the truth, and the life when he is a young man or woman, he may have to disregard his parents' wishes if they would force him to deny God's Word. Even in the family, we must obey God rather than men because no earthly authority can stand in the way of obeying the Lord. If earthly authority does not show the way to obedience, then it has lost its reason for existence; in fact, it has become demonic and must not be obeyed.

Listen to Christ's words: "Do not think that I have come to bring peace on earth; I have not come to bring peace, but a sword. For I have come to set a man against his father, and a daughter against her mother, and a daughter-in-law against her mother-in-law; and a man's foes will be those of his own household. He who loves father or mother more than me is not worthy of me; and he who loves son or daughter more than me is not worthy of me; and he who does not take his cross and follow me is not worthy of me" (Matt. 10:34–36; cf. Luke 12:51–53).

Christ is not against fathers loving their sons, or sons loving their fathers. Of course not—he commands them to love each other in spite of their imperfections. But fathers and sons must not consider their relationship the all-important thing. Christ is emphatically saying that his followers must be willing unconditionally to give up everything and everyone—including those of his own house—for the sake of the kingdom. If a man places love for father or mother above his love for Christ, then he has made a false god of his parent. Christ is warning his disciples that commitment to him is no little thing. The presence of sin and unbelief in the world means that bearing the cross will lead to division. In the last analysis the parent or child who rejects Christ within a Christian family is an enemy within the home.

One caution: obeying Christ does not mean rejecting parents, but rather refusing to adopt the basic antigod direction of their lives. Regretfully and painfully the young believer spiritually disaffiliates himself from the spirit that has captured his home.

The same principle applies to parents: they must not reject their children if they refuse to move in the direction of the kingdom of God. They must disapprove of the wrong walk of their children, but they are still their children and may not be rejected. Parents and children can accept and respect each other for what they are, despite basic disagreement, knowing that the fundamental matter can be corrected. Remaining open to each other is so essential that neither parents nor children may totally cut off the other. Only the Lord finally closes and opens the door.

The So-called Generation Gap

The so-called generation gap is a sign that in most homes a biblical view of nurture has lost out to the authoritarian-permissive view. The older generation is set on maintaining its authority; the younger generation is determined to undo all authority. This gap between the generations ought not to exist, yet it will continue to exist as long as nonbiblical views of nurture are in vogue.

The generation gap is not inherent in man's psyche, as many psychoanalysts and anthropologists contend. It actually arises from the false views of freedom and authority found in both the authoritarian and permissive families. As we have seen, it is just as unbiblical to blow up human authority into something absolute (authoritarianism) as it is to make human freedom absolute (permissiveness). Fathers and mothers will be reconciled with their children in the Lord if they realize that parents have their authority to ensure the freedom and responsible nurture of the children. In the body of Christ parents and children are united because the only decisive gap is between obedience to the Lord and disobedience. Parents and children who are not one in the faith have a real gap between them, a gap of heart confession rather than age. Only in Christ do the generations pull together (Mal. 4:6; Luke 1:17).

The Vulnerability of the Modern Family

No matter how faithfully parents follow the Lord they can run into real problems. For instance, the nuclear family can become a retreat from life rather than a haven in the midst of life. Parents feel the pressure of having to fill more roles than they can handle; the family becomes overdependent on TV, as a substitute for deep, satisfying contact with a wider group of people and as a way to forestall the loneliness of a faceless society. Except for superficial contact with others, too many families are completely closed off in themselves, either dedicated to fighting off the world and/or resigned to having a good time.

When the family withdraws to protect itself, it cannot provide the guidance and rest children need to prepare for life. The family itself suffers if it ignores the rest of society or pretends that it and its problems do not exist. For in actual fact, more than ever before the modern family is exposed to powerful influences it cannot control. Some families resist by banning TV, but then magazines, newspapers, and movies must go too! Where do parents draw the line? Must the school hide the realities of life? Should the church dwell only on the glories of heaven? Maybe a parent shouldn't even allow his children to have contact with other children who have already been "exposed"?

The fun-family is no better because it also is a form of withdrawal. Family fun is healthy, enjoyable, and necessary, but fun can also become such an idol that the family ignores the realities of life. Then their life together takes on a make-believe veneer because they have left the basic issues untouched. Withdrawing into the family citadel is a self-reflex which only intensifies the problems that caused the retreat in the first place.

Instead of preparing the child to face life and work for meaningful change as a person in his own right, withdrawal—for whatever reasons —subtly but inexorably teaches the child to conform and submit to the status quo. Since the family can't fully withdraw, retreat actually means that the family has to accept things as they are. In effect, the family becomes a powerful instrument by which society keeps prospective members in line. In such circumstances the family has surrendered its own birthright; it smothers rather than fosters authenticity and growth; it jeopardizes rather than encourages true meeting and sharing. In David Cooper's poignant phrase, the family becomes a "fur-lined bear trap."[3]

Today we are reaping the bitter fruit. Unwittingly, too many families kill troth rather than generate it. Families are being fractured. Mothers see their tasks as unrewarding and demeaning; they feel bored, alienated from the outside world, and frustrated at the disuse of their full talents. Fathers spend less and less time at home because the action and excitement are outside. Children and parents alike find each other and their home boring unless they are entertained by TV.

Family Outreach

However, the basic trouble is not with the nuclear family unit as such, but with the way we have misused it under the influence of distorting visions of life. Abolishing the family unit is not the answer. What we really need is new societal patterns that will allow families to be real families—places of troth and growth. Parents and children still need relative privacy if the family is to be family and fulfill its role in society. But it is time we realize that now that it has shed many of its nonessential functions, the family is extremely vulnerable. It must more clearly understand its relations to all the other segments of society because the family needs the active support of other families, single persons, the church, the school, business, the state, and so on to be a family.

The small nuclear family today requires more intensive interfamily contacts, including nonrelatives as well as relatives. Every child needs uncles and aunts. Grandparents, too, ought to be valued for their own contribution to family life instead of just being tolerated. The family needs to reach out to establish a network of relationships which can give it support. Families also need deep contacts with a small number of other families to know how others handle similar problems. Parents have to get over the habit of hiding their problems from each other. Rather than parading family achievements, much will be gained when parents share and discuss their common problems together.

Families also need the assurance that school and church are leading the children in the same direction they are going.[4] Families ought to demand that the political and economic, recreational and cultural areas develop in ways which promote healthy family life. Only in this way can we prevent young people from being pulled apart by the spirits of the age.

The family that closes in on itself and tries to be fully independent loses a great deal. In contrast, the family that feels part of a group of other families has a resiliency and ability to cope far beyond its own internal resources. A family that fosters outside relations no longer bears the pressure of making its inner relations fully sufficient. Consequently family troth has the space and freedom to develop. When a family opens its home to others who are lonely, it enlarges the horizons and increases the sensitivity of family members even as it helps meet another person's needs. The important point is that the contacts the family reaches for need to be deep ones rather than the superficial kind we've grown used to; otherwise, they will do little to deepen internal family relations.

One note of caution, however. Although the family's outreach is vitally important, it should not deprive the nuclear family of time for itself. Sometimes we use the need for outreach as an excuse to avoid facing our own family problems. The father may always be at meetings and the mother involved in church affairs. When they are at home together, they may have casual visitors or just talk superficially. Such a situation is generally just as bad as the isolated family. Outreach to escape has a compulsion about it that twists the help we offer into a manipulative and destructive tool.

New Family Patterns

No doubt new patterns of family living will be developed. Many talk of reviving the extended family or various kinds of communes. If such extended families can avoid the rigidity and patriarchal set-up of those in the nineteenth century, they indeed offer hope. If the communes can avoid the tribal set-up and allow each family its requisite privacy, they too are real possibilities. Two or three families, sharing a basic overriding vision about the meaning of life, could easily live together in quarters that combine private suites of rooms along with central communal recreation and dining areas. Since few such dwellings have been built to this point, and since many local zoning codes forbid them, couples who do share a common perspective in life and deep feeling for each other should seriously consider living near each other. For many families today this solution appears to hold the most promise.

Considering the wide range of living conditions—farm, suburb, or city—no one form of family living will best serve all the varying needs in the future. Space and location are not really the most important considerations, as the Japanese have discovered. Whatever forms develop, home must be a place of troth, adventure, and guidance. Forms which do not allow such homes to develop ought to be rejected. Thus, for example, the structure for the family argues against the one-parent or bachelor family as a normal phenomenon. Such arrangements are contradictions in terms because children need both male and female parents; they are the unfortunate victims when there is only one parent. In today's world the parents themselves need the support of the extended family and the community to fulfill their calling. One-parent families are not normal because family means father, mother, and children.

The "Working Mother"

The plight of the mother in today's family requires special attention. Since we don't often think of mothering as a calling of troth with the whole child's life at stake, it often becomes no more than endless dishwashing, picking up, making beds, cooking, dressing, and undressing the kids. In such a context the routines of housework are as dull and tedious as father's assembly-line drudgery. Surely mothers can be pardoned for not finding adequate meaning and fulfillment in these chores. Many mothers are going out to work to seek relief from sheer boredom.

First of all, it reveals male bias to consider this the mother's problem. Unfortunately many families begin with the assumption that it is clearly mother's duty to stay home and take care of the offspring. Why? Isn't the father as much a parent as the mother? He should be. Both father and mother are head of the family; father has no more authority than mother. Together they have the task and authority to raise a family. The question of the direction in which the family is to develop was decided when the couple married. Therefore, with a common understanding of their calling and task, the parents take up the challenge together. They need to realize the supreme importance of their task and the troth that characterizes fatherhood and motherhood. When both parents respect the office of parent they will even be able to find household chores satisfying because they're necessary to create a home where genuine nurture can best take place.

Together father and mother must decide how best to share the responsibilities of nurture. They should not assume that it is natural and God-willed for the woman to find her complete fulfillment in marriage and family while the man has an outside task to help him achieve fulfillment as a person. Being wife and mother does not exhaust womanhood any more than being husband and father exhausts manhood. A woman should also be able to follow a career even if she decides to marry and have children. Engaged couples need to discuss this delicate, highly important matter fully and openly. Husband and wife should agree on how each of them will combine his responsibilities as parent with those of his career. Furthermore, husbands-to-be should encourage their fiancées to train for a satisfying and long-term career. Since most mothers are still under forty when their children are teenagers, life-long vocation planning and training can help young women prevent the unnerving prospect of having virtually nothing worthwhile to do for the next thirty years.

In some families the father may be the proper person to stay home and take care of the family, even during the early years. However, it's more likely that mothers and fathers will both want to follow a career at some point in their lives. To be just, we need to find ways to reorganize our daily lives and our social patterns so that both parents have the opportunity to take up outside callings without endangering family life. More flexible work schedules would allow parents of preschool-age children to share their parental duties without loss of livelihood. A father or mother who wanted to make his parental office his primary profession should receive a salary. This would eliminate economic reasons for working outside the home. During pregnancy, women, and during childhood, one of the parents should be able to take an extended furlough without penalty. Mothers or fathers of school-age children should be able to have jobs that permit at least one of them to see their children off to school and welcome them home after school.

Many families are discovering that the mother's pursuit of outside interests makes her more attentive, understanding, and relaxed at home. Enjoying such experiences and growing through them, the mother develops herself more fully as a person. She is able to keep pace with her husband and growing family.

In any case, parents should share the routine as much as possible, both the mundane tasks of parenthood as well as the rewarding, stimulating, and pleasant tasks. Such sharing of the parental task would not only go a long way to help restore the true joys of motherhood, but it would also help many fathers discover new joys. The benefit for children is almost beyond words!

The family of the future can only survive as a community of bonded troth, as a mutual affair in which every member has the right to intimacy, support, understanding, and guidance. Within the family every member also has the calling to be intimate, supportive, understanding, and helpful. The family is not father's domain in which mother babysits and father terrorizes. Nor is it a playschool in which parents indulge and children manipulate. The family is a we-situation in which parents and children develop and grow into full persons through open and mutual sharing.

The Family—Not Alone

Although our temptation may be to turn the family into nothing, we also need to remember that it is not everything. The family does not stand alone because it is only one of the areas of the kingdom of God. Only the kingdom of heaven is all-inclusive; it alone asks for everything, and it alone can bear the strain of such demands.

The family is not everything. That is a sobering thought, but it is also comforting. For the last frontier is the kingdom of God, and that is a kingdom of grace. Our work as parents finds a sure foundation only in the faithfulness of God in his covenant. This grace gives parents the courage and strength to be responsible parents, capable of leading their children to the fear of the Lord. Only when parents remember that families have also been taken up in God's covenant and that by his grace they are doing his will, can they call on the children to obey, confident that they will.

The Father maintains his Word. Led by that Word the body of Christ is invulnerable before the gates of hell. This is comfort. Christ gave the keys of the kingdom to his people, to his church, to carry out all their tasks. In the family the keys of the kingdom are given to parents. Along with the keys the Lord gives the promise, "Truly, I say to you, whatever you bind on earth shall be bound in heaven, and whatever you loose on earth shall be loosed in heaven" (Matt. 18:18). If parents obey him in educating their children, they are obeying the Word; they can be sure that their obedience stands because the Word lives and stands forever. The Old Testament expresses the same thought in these words: "Train up a child in the way he should go, and when he is old he will not depart from it" (Prov. 22:6). If we are faithful in our families to his Word, we have the promise—sure in Jesus Christ—that our work will be blessed. What more can we ask? This means salvation for family life. As Proverbs exclaims so well: "Where there is no vision, the people perish: but he that keepeth the law, happy is he" (29:18, KJV).

105

NOTES

1. Three of the most comprehensive treatments of the abortion problem are Daniel Callahan's *Abortion: Law, Choice, and Morality* (London: Collier-Macmillan Ltd., 1970); John T. Noonan, ed., *The Morality of Abortion* (Cambridge: Harvard University Press, 1970); and R. F. R. Gardner, *Abortion: The Personal Dilemma* (Grand Rapids: Wm. B. Eerdmans, 1972).

2. George Peter Murdock's *Social Structure* (New York: Macmillan, 1949) set forth these functions and revived sociological interest in the universality of the family. Many have since disputed Murdock's claim; some have added "affection" as a fifth function. To my knowledge, all ignore or depreciate the troth-structure of the family.

3. David Cooper, *The Death of the Family* (New York: Random House, 1970), p. 4. Although justly reacting to the repressive character of many families and to society as a macrofamily, Cooper goes too far in claiming that the family must die if society is to solve its basic problems. In fact, Cooper's solution—a recovery of man's "self-containing autonomy" (p. 13)—is a refurbished version of the anti-God bias which is the root cause of society's ills.

4. In this context the importance of Christian day-school instruction for Christian families stands out. See, John Vriend *et al.*, *To Prod the Slumbering Giant* (Toronto: Wedge, 1972) for one Christian attempt to come to grips with the current educational crisis.

FRIENDSHIP: TRUST AND CONGENIALITY

Books and articles dealing with marriage and the family—whether to praise or debunk them—are almost innumerable. Friendship, however, is quite a different matter. Although hopeful signs appear now and then, the modern world generally ignores friendship. We admit that everyone needs a few friends, but we don't become very excited by their presence or absence. Today we rarely celebrate friendship.

Friendship Extolled

Although it is faring badly in the modern era, friendship was extolled in ancient times and to some extent in the Middle Ages. In the time of Plato and Aristotle friendship was considered the highest relationship. The perfect form of friendship represented the purest expression of the Greek love of the good and was the bond between two people who resembled each other in virtue. C. S. Lewis put it well: "Friendship seemed the happiest and most fully human of all loves, the crown of life and the school of virtue."[1]

Compared with marriage and family, friendship was the least natural, the least instinctive, and the least necessary relation; therefore, friendship appeared to rise above the concerns of passion, body, and emotion. Marriage and family ties were "natural," but friendship ties were "spiritual." Family bonds were instinctive, whereas marriage ties were thought to be largely economic, and the affection between husband and wife was simply passionate eros. As a state of mind, friendship could remain free of such "lower bodily" concerns. Since friends could be freely chosen, man was encouraged to lay aside the press of natural desires and enter the rational, divine, luminous realm of friendship.

The church met the new, idolized friendship head-on and grudgingly acknowledged the need to defend marriage and the family. However, the church was not really successful because friendship appealed to the ascetic, world-renouncing spirit which the church itself had encouraged during the Middle Ages. Later, when Renaissance men attempted to revive the ancient idolization of friendship, the church again became defensive. Under the influence of the Reformation, churchmen began to see friendship as the epitome of man's love for himself and potentially the competitor of love for God.

Because it was paganism that elevated friendship to such a high position, the church has seldom extolled its virtues. Even in humanistic circles, friendship has never regained the popularity it enjoyed in Grae-co-Roman times. Much of our indifference to friendship has grown out of the church's lasting influence and out of the modern obsession with physical sexuality. Even though little has been written about friendship since Aristotle's day, which has significantly advanced the discussion, the growing concern for authentic relationships suggests a renewed interest in friendship. Even the church is becoming involved in the discussion, as C. S. Lewis's chapter on friendship in *The Four Loves* indicates.

Friendship Depreciated

Despite a growing interest in better relationships, friendship for most people is an adolescent matter that largely ends with marriage. Not only is marriage no longer a form of friendship, but today friendship has become merely a prelude to marriage. Successful marriage puts an end to real friends. Of course, many married people are surrounded by large numbers of acquaintances, but to call them "friends" is to emasculate the word. Ordinarily, modern people are friendly as couples because we assume that legitimate friendships should stay within the confines of the family to avoid the danger of affairs and competition. Our slick movies and our after-dinner jokes about dad's night out suggest a genuine anxiety over the threat of outside contacts. The result is that today true friendships seldom occur. Very few sing the praises of friendship because very few have experienced its heights.

The Christian community is no exception. While a minority desire to see friendship renewed, the majority continue to ignore it. Little is written about the joys of friendship.[2] John Macquarrie's *Dictionary of Christian Ethics* treats an astonishing range of subjects but not friendship. And what has been written often suffers from the fact that friendship is considered only a "natural" love in contrast to the divine. The late Dutch Reformed ethicist, G. Brillenburg Wurth, wrote in 1953: "Friendship is certainly not one of the highest forms of love."[3] Similarly, Emil Brunner plays down friendship by declaring that it only foreshadows real community of agape. It is "the nearest approach of the natural spiritual element to *personal* community."[4] Even C. S. Lewis, whose comments on friendship are very helpful, believes friendship to be only a "natural" love, on a level with affection between parents and children and the eros between husband and wife. In Lewis's view these "natural" loves must strive toward charity, the divine love.

Given our disregard for friendship and the small number who actually have friends, whatever the Christian community can find to say about friendship must be said clearly and publicly. Especially two matters will concern us in this chapter. First, friendship is a good gift of the Lord which must be treasured and enjoyed. Second, friendship need not be rejected because of its questionable past. Every good thing is easily distorted and misused in this life. The Christian's task is to use friendship well, not to reject it out of hand. In the power of Christ's resurrection and under the leading of his Holy Spirit, the Christian community must lead the way in recovering the beauty of friendship as God intended from the beginning.

The Gift of Friendship

No man is an island. No man lives alone. By our very nature we belong together. We cannot live without human contact; every step of the way we rely upon our fellows. When troth becomes a live dimension of all these interrelations, they are occasions of authenticity, mutual sharing, and joy.

Marriage and the family, as we have already explored, are special ways in which man is called to troth and intimacy. Here troth is not simply one important dimension of the situation. It is the key to the relationships as a whole. Troth characterizes, constitutes, and qualifies such relations. One other special way to be intimate is friendship. Friendship is one of the three unique ways the Lord has given us which in a special way fill the human need for intimacy and troth. A man can make it through life without friends, but it is like a trip through a wilderness. For friendship is more than just rubbing shoulders; it is something special. As Francis Bacon observed: "For a crowd is not company, and faces are but a gallery of pictures; and talk but a tinkling cymbal where there is no love."[5]

All of us are involved in tightly structured relationships of authority and subordination. Besides these vertical relations, men also need to relate to one another horizontally as a matter of free choice. As C. S. Lewis put it, friends "meet like sovereign princes of independent states, abroad, on neutral ground, freed from our contexts."[6] Friends are equals.

Shared Congeniality

No one chooses his family, and once the marriage vow is taken the couple is bound for life. Friendships, however, can be freely formed anytime. Friendships begin from a certain attraction, an inner impulse which drives people together because they delight in each other's company. This psychic attraction or congeniality is the foundation for

110

friendship. It cannot be forced: either people are attracted to each other or they are not. Still, this sudden attraction is not yet friendship; it is merely the first spark which will eventually produce the flame of friendship. The congeniality of friendship makes it more open to variation and more flexible than marriage and family, which are physically and biotically founded.

Since many people feel guilty for liking some people and disliking others, we need to examine congeniality more closely. Emotional likes and dislikes are perfectly normal and ought to be accepted for what they are. All-important is what one does with his likes and dislikes. If they determine his conduct, he is acting unfaithfully. For example, a judge who miscarries justice because he likes the accused is guilty. The married man who has an affair with a pretty girl to whom he is attracted is also guilty. The customer who cheats the supermarket because he dislikes the manager is guilty, as is the woman who promotes an employee simply because she likes him. The point is that congeniality is indispensable for friendship, but it is not all there is to friendship, nor is it even the primary characteristic.

Once a mutual attraction between two people develops into a camaraderie involving common interests and concerns, a commitment of troth to each other can further deepen the relationship into friendship. Friendship is basically a moral matter, a matter of trust and intimacy, of give and take in troth.

The classical definitions of friendship (expressed by Plato, Aristotle, and Cicero[7]) recognized the importance of the psychic element in friendship; however, they also idolized the rational element. Unfortunately, this view is still adopted, even among Christians. When the rational replaces troth, with the freedom and relaxation it offers, friendship becomes little more than rational self-love.

Friendship Means Troth

Friendship occurs between two people who single each other out from other possible contacts; they treat each other specially and give mutually to each other. Friendship is reciprocal, preferential, and selective. Friendship is a pledged vow of troth between two persons based upon psychic congeniality. A relationship simply develops, matures, and slowly slides into friendship; troth takes time to develop. The vow of trust is usually unspoken, yet we all know our real friends. The moment we begin talking about friendship something seems to be lost. No friend needs to be reminded of his promise! Even if my friend and I are working at the same task, we don't become selfishly competitive. I wish him the best, and when he is successful, I share his happiness and rejoice in it almost as much as he.

Friendship is exuberant, spontaneous, and tender. Friends support one another and count on one another; they even begin to think alike. A friend can be called on for help, but we are almost embarrassed to trouble him in this way. For when a friend sees a problem, he offers help, but he doesn't want it mentioned. He only did what a true friend does. No one deliberately treats a friend shabbily, but he understands when we do. We treasure a good friend. When we say to ourselves, "He is worth his weight in gold," the old cliché takes on real meaning for us. A person has only a few such friends, if that many, in his entire life. As Francis Bacon exclaims, a friend "doubles a man's joy and cuts his sorrow in half."[8]

On the other hand, a friend says his piece; he doesn't automatically approve of everything we do or say, and we take it because we know it is for our good. As Solomon put it, "Faithful are the wounds of a friend; but the kisses of an enemy are deceitful" (Prov. 27:6, KJV). Face to face and heart to heart friends affect each other and grow. "Iron is made the finer by iron," exclaims Proverbs 27:17 (JB), "man is refined by contact with his neighbour." Friendship involves mutual confidence, trust, effort, and devotion. As George Washington said to his nephew, friendship is a "plant of slow growth."

Friends do not attempt to control each other because they respect each other too much. Friends give of themselves, for only in mutual self-giving can trust and friendship prosper. Holding back in order to control the situation and manipulate a friend kills troth and deepens loneliness. Friends can accept anything from each other—except a break in troth. The only injury to a friend is mistrust, which will end the friendship if it is not corrected. Ecclesiasticus says it beautifully:

> If you have drawn your sword on a friend,
>> do not despair; there is a way back.
> If you have opened your mouth against your friend,
>> do not worry; there is hope for reconciliation;
> but insult, arrogance, betrayal of secrets, and
> the stab in the back—
>> in these cases any friend will run away (Sirach 22:21–27, JB).

David makes the same point:

> Were it an enemy who insulted me,
>> I would put up with that;
> had a rival got the better of me,
>> I could hide from him.
> But you, a man of my own rank,
>> a colleague and a friend,
> to whom sweet conversation bound me
>> in the house of God! (Ps. 55:12–14, JB).

Sure Friends

If the trust remains unbroken, the troth between friends grows. If friends share common goals, purposes, and beliefs, this commonly held vision serves to open up, fulfill, and integrate the relation. The result is the exquisite phenomenon of a *fast* friend, tried and true, who sticks closer than a brother. This kind of friend is faithful, even unto death. James 2:23 reports that Abraham was the "friend of God" (cf. 2 Chron. 20:7 and Isa. 41:8). Christ himself said to his disciples, "No longer do I call you servants, . . . but I have called you friends, for all that I have heard from my Father I have made known to you" (John 15:15). Ecclesiasticus puts it all together.

> A faithful friend is a sure shelter,
>> whoever finds one has found a rare treasure.

A faithful friend is something beyond price,
  there is no measuring his worth.
A faithful friend is the elixir of life,
  and those who fear the Lord will find one.
Whoever fears the Lord makes true friends,
  for as a man is, so is his friend (Sirach 6:14—17, JB).

Forms of Friendship

Friendship is a gift of the Lord. The structure for friendship—a mutual promise of troth founded on congeniality—is constant and inviolable. Whether good or bad, all friendships live under this norm and are responses to this norm. At the same time the forms of friendship can be as diverse as the possibilities of creation and the people who form them. Since friendship occurs between individuals who have no authority over one another as friends, the faces or forms of friendship vary more widely than in most other relationships. Young and old can be friends. Friendship can cross ethnic boundaries. Although more complicated, friendship can even spring up between people who are on an equal footing in one situation and an unequal footing in another, as in the case of a minister and a sheriff, for instance.

Friendship can be shared with a third or fourth party because it is fussy and choosy, but not exclusivistic. Lovers are engrossed in each other's company face to face; friends are shoulder-to-shoulder open to a new friend. For the unmarried, genuine friendship can provide the solace and intimate sharing they otherwise so often miss.

Cross-sex Friendships

Although our sex-crazed society has made it difficult for many of us to handle them, male-female friendships are perfectly legitimate. Once we have distinguished the different structures for marriage and friendship, we no longer need to see the one as a competitor of the other.

Relieved of the impossible burden of being forced to fulfill all human desires and needs by itself, each relationship in fact can help and support the other. A married man can be friends with another woman, married or unmarried, provided that they both know that the relationship is friendship and not marriage. Enriched through their friendship, each has more to give to their other relationships.

Knowing the difference between marriage and friendship is of vital importance to all of us. Men and women do desire to relate to each other and become close. We do need and want to share intimacy and understanding. But for many of us this natural desire never has a chance to develop because we are haunted by the idea, common currency in our society, that being close always leads to the bedroom. That idea is simple, unadulterated nonsense. But it has its pernicious effect, and we retreat and are afraid to be close.

If we are married, we really don't dare relate to a member of the opposite sex because—so the myth goes—it inevitably undermines our marriage. If we are not married, genuine relating is no easier. Both parties—so the myth goes—are only motivated by their desire for physical intimacy. They too are victims. Physical intimacy may be easy and quick, but by itself it is a far cry from genuine human sharing in troth and leaves you only more lonely and disturbed.

The myth that all close contact necessarily leads to physical intercourse is just that—a myth. We must free ourselves from its deadening influence. Friendship is a God-given way to be intimate which does not involve physical intercourse. Of course, casual physical contact does play a role in friendship. But such physical contact always retains its limited role. If the physical begins to demand more room, if the desire for physical intercourse awakens and deepens in the friendship of a man or woman already married (or of two men or two women), a difficult, antinormative situation is developing because the friends are not obeying the norm for friendship. Sometimes such friendships have to be terminated. Intensive physical desire ending in intercourse is not a part of friendship simply because friendship is not marriage. Friends who experience such desire have a clear indication that something is wrong with their friendship. Even though friendship can lead to other kinds of relationships—some good and some bad—the distinction between them remains valid. Rather, when we say that friendship had led to marriage, for example, we recognize that friendship is one thing and marriage another.

Adolescent Friendships

So far we have been talking largely about friendship in its mature form. For a moment we should consider the adolescent, schoolboy friendships we all have enjoyed. Such relations lack the depth and stability of mature friendship but are crucial for youngsters in every developmental stage in life. These peer relationships function as a God-appointed way for children to begin to relinquish their childhood dependence on the family. Through them boys and girls learn to relate to peers, broaden their life experience, and grow. Such friendships are easily made and just as easily broken. Older youngsters find it more difficult to form friendships, but those made are relatively lasting. Boys and girls "cross their hearts and hope to die" if they are not faithful to each other, a pledge they often seal in blood. The next moment they forget about it and betray the oath. One minute they are arm in arm, the next at each other's throats. Such freedom and ease with relationships is just part of the process of maturing. Since they cannot yet establish the deeper kind of troth involvements we have been discussing, we cannot expect a stick-closer-than-a-brother relationship among youth.

Adolescent friendships are indispensable if the child is to know himself and to relate to others. Young people are generally bound together because they enjoy the same activities and they live near one another. Thus, children can be greatly disturbed if they move away from their old friends, yet a month later new friends have driven the others from their minds.

Mature friendships tend to be just the other way around. Separation from a real friend grows more painful as time moves on. Adolescent friendships are an important part of growing up, but they should serve as preparation for the mature friendship of adulthood, as well as for all of life's involvements.

Courtship and Friendship

Courtship leading to marriage is one of the relations that slowly develops from adolescent friendships. Generally couples do not and should not decide to marry because they have a physical desire for each other. Rather they should be delighted and psychically overwhelmed by each other as whole persons. They get to know each other better and soon become friends. If the friendship intensifies and physical desire for each other awakens as part of the growing intimacy, they have the beginnings of courtship. In other words, if they begin to need tender caresses and ardent embraces instead of casual physical contact, the couple is involved in courtship, not simply the friendship of youth.

Friends and Companions

No doubt the troth of friendship seems unreal to many of us. Our friends are not that way. Actually, many of the people we call friends are not truly friends in the way we have described. We also know "fair-weather" friends, who are like shadows that appear in fair weather and vanish on a rainy day. There are "temporary" friends who disappear once the events that led them to be friends are over. Sometimes we even give the name "friend" to anyone who is not our enemy. That is simply nonsense.

Many good acquaintants, relatives, business partners, and comrades-in-arms are not really friends. There is nothing wrong with such a situation. Everyone needs and requires a whole network of such contacts, but we should not delude ourselves into thinking that they are friends. For in so doing, we deprive ourselves of the special treat of real friendship. With all these people we may have easy, cordial relations, tinged with affection; but we do not have the mutual promise of troth. Of course, camaraderie may lead to real friendships. Indeed, such contacts are the matrix in which friendship blossoms and flourishes. Yet we must distinguish socially qualified comradeships from friendship as an ethically qualified relation of troth. Two persons confronted with particular tasks become companions, bound together by the interests or tasks they share. Such relations are usually confined to definite functions, so that when the task ends the acquaintanceship expires a natural death. Students working at a summer resort, the members of a civic committee, actors in a play—all are companions until their particular job ends. That is why class reunions are often so disappointingly boring and awkward. There is really nothing to say to each other once the magic of the school days is gone.

The Scriptures distinguish between comrades and friends (although most translations do not convey the difference). Proverbs 18:24 is often translated: "He that makes many friends does it to his destruction, but there is a friend that sticks closer than a brother." However, the Hebrew uses two different words for *friend*, a distinction that the New English Bible captures: "Some companions are good only for idle talk, friends stick closer than a brother."

No Friends—Why?

Most of us would like to call all our associates friends for the simple, but sad reason that we do not have real friends. We like to console ourselves with many comrades to hide the lack of real friends. There are many reasons for this unhealthy state of affairs. Friendship is usually given step-motherly treatment—viewed as a lower concern, accused of being a competitor of marriage and the family, identified with love of neighbor, and often simply ignored.

118

Not a Lower Concern

Friendship has too often received step-motherly treatment because it is considered a "natural" love over against the "spiritual" love of God. In brief, it is said, friendship belongs to this world; the love of God is in the higher realm of the kingdom of God.

This perspective and the nature-grace dualism from which it springs is alien to the Gospel. The Scriptures teach that no area of creation is excluded from the kingdom of Jesus Christ. Every part of life must be renewed in his name. Every human relationship—friendship, marriage, family, state, school, and so on—has its own created place in that kingdom. Thus, when we speak of "natural" loves (friendship, family, and marriage) in contrast to the "spiritual" love of God, we suggest that the love of God is above this world in some higher realm and therefore outside the kingdom of Christ. Such a view leaves the Christian with nothing to say in the so-called natural areas, where the love of God apparently cannot be manifested. At the very best, such love can only be foreshadowed. Thus Christians become uneasy because these natural relations, into which all of us must enter, appear to be lower concerns, alien to the spirit. Furthermore, natural relations seem to steal valuable time from the only legitimate concerns: seeking the spiritual things which are above.

The Christian community needs to realize the crippling affect of dividing creation into a natural and a spiritual realm.[9] That division allows men to see some parts of life as sacred and therefore better, while others are secular and less valuable. To accept a basic nature-grace division is to deny the unity of creation, reaffirmed in redemption. Unless we recognize the unity of the creation, we will be unable to give friendship its intended place in human life, for it will always have to compete with love of God.

Dividing life into things natural and spiritual is contrary to the basic thrust of the Scriptures. When Paul told the Colossian believers to seek the things that are above where Christ is, he did not urge them to leave the world. On the contrary, he called them to live in a spiritual way in all of life's relationships. *Spiritual* does not refer to an additional, higher realm; instead, it describes a life in its totality driven, motivated, and guided by the love of God. If all our relations are spiritual—driven by the love of God—there must be a place for genuine, renewed friendships. The only important question we need to ask about a particular friendship is whether it is moved by the love of God or gripped by the lie of the Devil.

Love is the summary and unity of the Word of God. When the Holy Spirit opens our hearts to God's love in Christ, we are redeemed and set right in relation to his Word. Man responds to Christ's redemption by obeying the various words of the Lord for life, which together constitute the Word. For instance, the Lord has given us a word for friendship, as well as for marriage, family, and all other relations. It is these law-words of the Lord that make friendships, marriages, and families possible.

Since friendship is a possibility only because of God's Word, we may not call it *natural* to devaluate it. Rather, one of the ways to love the Lord is to be good, faithful friends. In this way the structural dualism between natural loves and the love of God disappears.

Friendship and Love of Neighbor

Unfortunately, Christians have seldom thought of friendship itself as spiritual, as a way of showing the love of God. Many have felt that selecting one person or another as a close friend degraded friendship to a natural lower concern. Thus, to save friendship for the Christian church, many have read the biblical mandate to love your neighbor as yourself as the Christian idea of friendship. Others have confused or identified friendship with the idea of brotherhood and sisterhood in Christ. Both views lose the unique nature of friendship in the mud of confusion.

If we confuse and identify friendship with Christ's central command to love one another, we have to conclude that all of life's activities are to be normed by the model of friendship. We are called to be friends with everyone. This attitude often surfaces in the American aphorism "Be nice today." But this leads to insurmountable problems. No one can have a special relationship with every person he meets. Can friendship rather than justice determine the court's rulings? Are children basically their parents' friends? Can businesses develop primarily to do favors for friends? Friendship simply cannot become the central model for all of life. If it does, the relation will either become vacuous, innocuous, and unexciting or it will take on the dimensions of some other relation.

When we confuse friendship with the love of neighbor or with the humanist doctrine that all men are brothers, we reduce friendship to a meaningless phrase. If everyone is my friend, I can no longer have a friendship that is special and selective.

The result is obvious: if everyone is my friend, no one is my friend. The idea of comrades in the Communist world is one example of this distortion. The idea of homogenized and bland friends of Western democracies is another.

To claim every neighbor as a tried and true friend or to treat other relations as forms of friendship is to level out the diversity of society into a colorless and tasteless uniformity. In that kind of climate genuine friendship seems disgusting, and any relationship that cannot be subsumed under friendship seems suspicious.

Friendship and Marriage

If we merge friendship and love, we cannot correctly relate friendship and marriage.[10] If friendship and love are identical, we must conclude that marriage is a form of friendship, or it is not a love relation at all. The second alternative can be ignored since the great majority certainly believe marriage is a relationship of love. Marriage, then, must be a form of friendship. But that conclusion opens up countless questions. May I treat every friend as a husband or wife, or may I only have one real friend, that is, a husband or wife? Both possibilities are deeply disturbing. Today people answer yes to the first question, just as often as in the past many answered yes to the second question.

If marriage is a form of friendship, it can either be just another form of friendship or a special form. If marriage is just one form of friendship among others, friends should be free to play husband and wife whenever they feel like it. If the husband-wife union is no different than a friend-friend alliance, marriage loses its special character. Perhaps, then, marriage ought to be a special form of friendship. In that case, marriage would become an especially intense friendship that serves as the model, goal, or paradigm of all friendships. Every friendship, if it blossoms and blooms, should end up like a marriage. The implications of this position are equally uncomfortable. Either friendship is legitimate only as a preparation for marriage or marriage gives up its exclusive character so that every friendship can develop into a marriage.

Given its desire to protect marriage, no wonder the Christian church ended by devaluating friendship. The results, however, are coming back to haunt us today. Reducing friendship to a path to marriage virtually condemns people to only one genuine human contact—his or her spouse. If a married person maintains friendships, they could intensify and begin to compete with the marriage (the special friendship one already has). Therefore, any unmarried person who maintains a deep contact with married people is suspect and possibly promiscuous.

As many are discovering, marriage suffers severe strain if it is the only possibility for real sharing and inner contact. Since most marriages can't take the extra strain, husband and wife themselves remain strangers to each other and intensely lonely. When stress develops, outside liasons look especially tempting. What's worse, the unmarried are doomed to miss out on the companionship of the married and vice versa.

Thus, our zeal to protect marriage from the attacks common in our century has gotten out of hand. We hedge marriage in so thoroughly that we weaken it and cut it off from both the stimulation and the support which the partners could find with other people.

We need to recognize the God-willed possibility of friendship being friendship; marriage, marriage; and family, family. Certainly in actual living they are linked to one another, but this very intertwinement reveals that the contours of the husband-wife relation are not identical with those of father-mother and friend-friend relations. Troth plays a key role in all three relationships, but the troth in marriage is different from the troth in friendship and the troth in family.

Since each of these relations is unique, none can be defined in terms of the others. Neither can marriage, family, and friendship become all there is to life, for the uniqueness of these relations also involves limitations. Thus Christ's central command to love God and our neighbor cannot be reduced to, say, friendship. Friendship is to be *one* way in which we love God and our neighbor; marriage and family are other ways. Friendship must not be made everything, but neither must it be nothing.

Unfortunately, confusing love and friendship not only deprives friendship of its special meaning but it also hollows out the meaning of Christ's love-Command. To love your neighbor as yourself does not simply mean to befriend everyone. Friendship is only one of the many ways to love the Lord and neighbor. We hesitate to read Christ's words as "Love God and your *friends* as yourself"; yet that is essentially what we do when we reduce the idea of "neighbor" to "friend." We arbitrarily shrink the central thrust of Christ's command unless we think of neighbor as all fellow-humans who are called in every way to be image-bearers of the Lord. "Love your neighbor" is a call to do everything to help him serve the Lord.

Similarly, the biblical call to love our enemies does not mean simply being nice to them, trusting them as friends, letting them do whatever they desire. Critics pick up that moralistic reduction as evidence that Christianity is idealistic and impossible. That attack would be justified if the be-nice approach actually got at the point of Christ's command, but it misses the whole point. Whatever else they might be, enemies are still men who must be helped in every possible way to become co-workers in God's kingdom. Loving our enemies means showing, them how to be obedient to the Word of life. As the occasion demands, we may have to resort to many apparently cruel things, such as punishing or resisting. Love of neighbor—including enemies—must not be reduced to mawkish sentimentality or fawning friendship. Love of neighbor involves the central drive and motive force which is to guide us in all our relations. Friendship is one important way to give concrete form to our love for our neighbor, but friendship is not big enough to include loving our enemies.

Brotherhood and Sisterhood in Christ

Friendship is one way to be a neighbor to your fellowmen. Another way is to be a fellow confessor. In the Christian church this takes on the form of fellowship between believers in Christ. We lose much of God's intended satisfaction when we confuse the idea of brothers in fellowship and the idea of friends.

By its nature, friendship is selective, preferential, and based on shared congeniality. Unless we water down the meaning of *friend*, we have to admit that there are far too many Christians to call everyone a friend. Moreover, each of us knows many staunch Christians with whom we have no special desire to strike up a friendship. Fellow Christians are personally not always compatible. That in itself is not wrong. It all depends on what happens from there on. If friends are given special privileges in the worship community, and others are ignored or looked down upon, things are in a bad way. Although not everyone need or can be one's friend, everyone can and ought to be a fellow confessor of Christ. And every fellow confessor must be treated with brotherly love —as the Apostle urges time and again (Rom. 12:10; 1 Thess. 4:9; 2 Pet. 1:7; cf. Heb. 13:1). Brothers and sisters in Christ must join in encouraging one another, in mutual support and help. They must always be willing to offer a helping hand and a cup of cold water to anyone in distress—for the sake of the Gospel.

If one suffers under the notion that every fellow Christian ought to be his friend, he is either bound to have a bad conscience because so few are his friends or he has no real idea of the special nature of friendship. And he still has a bad conscience because he can't contact enough people. Moreover, if the notion of being brothers and sisters in confessing Christ is regarded as basically a matter of personal friendship, the worship community tends to turn into a gathering of friends or a social club. In such instances the focus on together listening to the Word in its central thrust and the confessional communal response is lost or illegitimately minimized. Everyone is our neighbor; many are our brothers in Christ; a few may also be our friends.

Cliques

Friendship can be lost through confusion or identification with some other relation. But friendship can also be perverted by inflation. Sometimes friends form cliques that turn in on themselves to the exclusion of everyone else. The clique overflows the bounds of friendship and attempts to swallow up all other relationships by becoming a privileged circle serving itself—an elite that doesn't care what anyone else does, says, or thinks.

The clique emasculates true friendship for the sake of selfish pride. Cliques offer the prestige of belonging to the ruling coterie, of obtaining positions of esteem and honor, of having the privileges of power. Personal growth, troth, and enrichment—the plant of friendship—are choked by the weeds of corporate haughtiness and self-aggrandizement. The group exists for the group, a self-elected aristocracy. Everyone outside the circle must be reminded frequently that is not in it.

The common distortions of friendship depend upon each other and are often found together. Even as the clique parades its factional haughtiness, it exhorts the masses to recognize that everyone is a comrade. For example, a well-known figure in the community praises the public school system but sends his own children to private schools. By exciting the masses to become brothers, united for God and country, the elite stymie

125

the formation of potential countergroups and consolidate their own position even more. Such false friendships so misuse the relationship that they become tyrannical.

Friendship in the Kingdom

If friendship is kept in place—neither idolized to haughtiness nor leveled-out to blandness—it is an invaluable gift of God that enriches and deepens human life. In its proper dimensions, friendship holds the promise of deep joy and true understanding. The kingdom of God provides the possibility for putting things in the place God provided for them at the creation. Only the vision of that kingdom allows us to see all things in their proper relation—without in principle elevating one matter at the expense of others. Thus, we can experience the wholeness, liberty, and integration in our life which is the very meaning of salvation in Jesus Christ.

No Room for Friendship

We have explored a manifold of reasons why friendship is not flourishing in our time. But there is one more reason, at least as weighty as all the other put together: the state of our society.

In our technomatic society man no longer has to struggle to survive, but paradoxically, technology's cold hardware has become the altar where modern man sacrifices his humanity to the gods of efficiency, technology, money, and physical sexuality. He likes what technology offers, but he can't help feeling a victim of the political and economic forces which surround him.

American families move so often that few have time to make fast friends. A year or two abroad or even a few months of isolation at home can make us realize just how rapidly neighborhoods, cities, and even the marketplace change. The competitive drive to make more money and to collect more "tangible assets" keeps many people so busy that they have to abandon any idea of friendships. For these reasons, among others, Americans often admit to feeling out-of-touch with other people, alienated from American life, and reduced to a part of a faceless mass.

There seems to be so little room or time for human feeling and compassion, for sharing and togetherness. Troth, openness, authenticity, warmth, integrity, sensitivity, understanding, commitment seem to be only words. Manipulation, double-dealing, efficiency, coldness, emptiness, suffocation, loneliness, and alienation appear to be the realities. For many people television has become the main substitute for continuous companionship. Blandness is the order of the day in human relations. Vance Packard calls us a "nation of strangers."[11] And where there is so little genuine human sharing, so little authenticity and integrity, there is little fuel for friendship.

If in this tumbleweedlike existence a man's longing for contact overcomes his fear of contact, he had better not look to society for help. Our society doesn't realize the God-willed possibility of a variety of human relations, each with its own structure, freedom, responsibility, and special satisfactions. With few disclaimers, most of us believe or at least act as if we believe that under the façade of a network of social relationships, we are basically animals competing in a sexual jungle in which only the rich survive. Since few can risk opening up and sharing in such a competitive climate, most of us protect ourselves by either joining the battle or withdrawing altogether. The price is the same whatever the choice: loneliness.

It is an ironic critique of our society that even this loneliness is being exploited for economic gain. "Purveyors of human contact" hold out the promise of intimacy in talk shows, encounter groups, nude marathons, telephone companions, dating services, and so on. But instant intimacy is just a bad joke.

The kind of leisurely friendships recorded in the diaries and novels of the eighteenth and nineteenth centuries just aren't possible today. Society just does not allow the freedom for the growth and development of genuine friendships. Two men, who become friendly, are assumed to be homosexual; two women are lesbians, or at least conspirators in breaking their marriages. And, of course, any man and woman together are on an affair. Obviously, none of this is true. Out of fear we have done away with kisses, tears, and tenderness—none of which really signifies anything out of the ordinary. Stranger indeed is their absence in daily life. In our society we have been conditioned so thoroughly that we Christians also suspect such relationships of being at least latently homosexual, lesbian, or adulterous. No one waits for proof before labeling. In fact, anyone who asks for proof is likely to get only a jeer: "Well, what do you expect? Do you think they'd do it in public?"

What a world to live in! We need and long for comfort but are afraid to be intimate because of the fear that it can only end up as physical intercourse. What could be more paralyzing! And if the situation is not dreary enough, today we are incessantly urged to take advantage of our "real natures" and discover that physical sexuality is itself intimacy. What lies!

Intimacy is impossible without commitment. Without inner contact with other people, nothing human takes place. And friendship is a human community. It cannot be programmed to flourish.

We seldom realize what a tragic loss we experience when we do without friendship. The loss is particularly great for those who, for one reason or another, lack the comfort and joy of intimacy that troth brings to marriage and family. To deprive the unmarried of genuine friendship is to condemn them to a life of aching loneliness and pain which others cannot even imagine. For them friendship could mean a bounteous share in the spice and joy of life. For many it could even mean the difference between experiencing life as a cruel trick or a rare treat. The Christian community faces its obligation actively to promote conditions that will allow true friendship to flourish, with an urgent cry and a whispered prayer.

Troth must be recovered. Only then will authenticity and integrity again flourish in the land. Only then will the special troth intimacies of marriage, family, and friendships flourish. For when troth is not a live dimension of the human situation, it is unrealistic to expect the miracle of troth even in marriage, family, or friendship. Marriage, family, and friendship cannot long continue to be islands of troth in a hostile climate. If people rarely count on each other's word in daily life, how can the relations in which counting on each other is everything hope to survive? Our culture requires a new life-style—a biblical life-style—in which keeping troth is an essential mark.

NOTES

1. C. S. Lewis, *The Four Loves* (London: Fontana Books, 1960), p. 35.

2. M. C. D'Arcy, *Mind and Heart of Love* (New York: Meridian Books, 1959). D'Arcy regarded friendship as the perfection of love. See also Andrew M. Greeley, *The Friendship Game* (New York: Doubleday, 1970) and Ignace Lepp, *The Ways of Friendship* (New York: Macmillan, 1966).

3. G. Brillenburg Wurth, *Gestalten der Liefde* (Kampen: Kok, 1953), p. 138.

4. Emil Brunner, *The Divine Imperative* (Philadelphia: Westminster Press, 1947), p. 519. Other writers also consider friendship basically incompatible with the commandment of love. For instance, see S. Kierkegaard's, *Works of Love* (New York: Harper Bros., 1962), pp. 59, 65, 133–34 and A. Nygren, *Agape and Eros* (London: S.P.C.K., 1957).

5. Francis Bacon, *Essays* XXVII Of Friendship. (New York: Odyssey Press, 1937), p. 76.

6. Lewis, *Four Loves*, p. 66.

7. Even though Aristotle realized that friends must be loyal to one another, he also founded friendship on self-love. Plato already knew that the psychic element was very important in friendship, but he turned this indispensable element into the dominant feature and called it egocentric desire. Aristotle realized that Plato had been wrong. Friendships of utility and pleasure do have this egocentric thrust, but friendship proper is a rational friendship for the good. Both Plato and Aristotle made the whole matter much too logical. For Plato friendship demanded mental steadiness and control of the psychophysical; the

good, he argued, is known through reason, and friendship must serve the good. Aristotle stressed the need to develop a rational habit of just proportion, incorporating lower desires. Plato considered friendship basically a rational-psychic matter, and Aristotle basically a rational-legal affair. For Aristotle see *Nicomachean Ethics* VIII (Cambridge: Harvard University Press, 1926), for Plato his *Lysis* in *The Dialogues of Plato*, vol. 1, trans. B. Jowett (New York: Scribner, Armstrong, and Co., 1878). Cicero summed up the ancient tradition in a definition which is still widely held: "A perfect conformity of opinions upon all religious and civil subjects, united with a highest degree of mutual esteem and affection." *Essay on Friendship* in *Cicero's Offices* (New York: Everyman's Library, 1966), p. 177.

8. Bacon, *Essays* XXVII Of Friendship, p. 79.

9. For the different types of two-realm theories and the problematics involved, see my essay "Must the Church Become Secular?" in *Out of Concern for the Church* (Toronto: Wedge, 1970).

10. Greeley's book on friendship is a recent case in point. "Love and friendship are the same thing" (p. 33), and yet marriage is the "model and root of all human friendship" (p. 35).

11. Vance Packard, *A Nation of Strangers* (New York: McKay, 1972).

EPILOGUE

TROTH: A CALL TO FREEDOM

When the Lord calls us to troth, he opens the way before us for real intimacy in our marriages, our families, and our friendships. Though such intimacy may disturb some, most of us should be reassured. Undoubtedly the Lord's call also strengthens our determination to work at the relationships we have with other people. Yet in our zeal to live more faithfully, we can forget that the Lord's call to intimacy is a call to freedom. At the best, it opens up human life to the joy and satisfaction of the deep relationships God intended man to enjoy. At the very least, the Lord's norms for human relations offer the kind of liberating insight that suddenly focuses on what has gone wrong in our own lives.

Diagnosis is a liberating experience for all of us because it forces half-hidden problems out into the open where we can deal with them. Problems that remain vague and murky can so threaten us that we feel overwhelmed at their enormity. However, insight into what God intended life to be can show us what went wrong, in our childhood home for instance. We no longer have to feel that our home life was totally bad because the problem is cut down to size. People who learn to locate their family problems and to assess them in accurate proportion often find their bitterness toward their parents melting away.

For husbands and wives, too, locating the problem can be liberating rather than threatening. Couples who have not isolated their problems often find themselves dogged by the growing fear that their marriage is headed for total breakdown. Hearing the Lord's Word for troth in marriage puts such couples at least three steps ahead: they see what constitutes a healthy marriage; they begin to recognize the diverse causes of marital breakdown; and they discover that trouble in one part of their marriage need not lead to total breakdown. Such understanding takes the threat out of marriage and replaces it with real liberation.

Men and women who learn to respond to God's call to troth will find freedom from the pressure to emulate a current hero or an eminent married couple. Instead of living according to a specific community model—whether it's one projected in the media, in the pulpits, or even by the local patriarchs—each couple, each family, and each set of friends is free in the Lord to make their own unique response to God's call.

Anyone who has lived with the tyranny of a "perfect" model knows how welcome such freedom would be. Unlike parents, spouses, or friends, the Lord never greets us with, "My mother never did it that way —I thought you were like her." Or, "What's the matter with you? Grown men don't cry!" Or, "Why can't you get good grades like your cousin? She's such a good student."

We all know how frustrating such advice can be. We want to please, but we know we can never really be like someone else. Constant reminders that we don't measure up to someone else's behavior effectively undermine our sense of worth and identity. When we admit to ourselves that we can't measure up to other people's standards, we usually face two alternatives: we can stop trying to keep up with the local hero and withdraw from all who pressure us to shape up, or we can carefully construct a mask in an attempt to be someone else.

When we adopt other people's lives as a pattern for our own, we lose the freedom to develop the kinds of responses that fit our own talents and spirits. On the other hand, the person who is elevated to a norm also suffers. Since "norms" never make mistakes, he must always be on display. Frequently, he has to cover up the weaknesses he knows only too well. Inevitably, he suffers under the tension of knowing his fabricated life might fall apart at any moment.

The Lord's norms for human life deliver us from the tyranny of local paragons and the ghosts of the past. We need to guard the freedom Christ gives us when he calls us to develop ourselves and our relationships in response to his Word. Neither exemplary conduct nor apparent success can become our norm. Instead we ought to see through the good marriages, the happy families, and the firm friendships to the norm that invited such responses in the first place.

When we learn to respect the unique character of marriage, family, and friendship, we also find liberation. For instance, our desire to be good parents can so absorb us that marriage and friendship seem less important and therefore less worthy of our time. Parents really don't need to feel guilty when they take time for themselves. In fact, once they see that marriage and family are mutually supportive instead of competitive, they will safeguard that time even more carefully.

Husbands and wives can find the same freedom when they discover that outside friendships can support marriages rather than destroy them. If men and women recognize the difference between marriage and friendship, they can relate to each other freely, knowing that intimacy between friends doesn't have to lead to the bedroom. A husband and wife who are unable to draw the boundaries clearly will find themselves paralyzed and unable to form deep friendships if they care about their marriage at all. Those who believe the modern myth that physical sex is the way to intimacy will find themselves the losers. Although they may overcome their fear of relating to other people, they soon discover that physical intimacy does not fully satisfy. On the other hand, God's call to men and women is intensely liberating, for it is a call to friendships and to other relations in which the physical has only a very limited place.

One last comment. Knowing that we are responding to God's call when we marry, have children, and form friendships also gives us real hope in times of difficulty. God promises to be near us if we hold on to his Word. He encourages us to work at keeping troth; he will give the blessing. The psalmist's prayer catches the hope of the relationship:

I PLEDGE YOU MY TROTH

I have chosen the way of fidelity,
>I have set my heart on your rulings.
I cling to your decrees:
>Yahweh, do not disappoint me.
I run the way of your commandments,
>since you have set me free (Ps. 119:30–32, JB).

AN APPENDIX: PAUL ON WOMEN[1]

Although Paul's teachings on women are not strictly within the limits of this book, they deserve careful study because so many people believe the Apostle taught that women should be subordinate to men. Generally speaking, commentators draw that conclusion because they slight God's order for creation or they believe the Fall replaced the original order with disorder. When expositors ignore the creation motive, their later exegesis is inevitably affected.[2] As a result, interpreters too easily assume that Paul faces a dilemma: either a unisex position (the Gnostic equalization of men and women) or the subordination and inequality of women (Judaic and Hellenistic teaching).

Confronted by these two alternatives, the majority decide that Paul taught the subordination of women. Once they make that choice, commentators have a relatively easy time finding support for male superiority in Paul's references to the creation. However, Paul's comment in Galatians 3:28 causes real problems: ". . . there is neither male nor female; for you are all one in Christ Jesus." Those who believe that Paul taught the superiority of men must defuse this passage either by neglecting it or by accusing Paul of giving in to Gnostic influence. Some falsely spiritualize the passage, claiming that men and women are equal only on the spiritual level, in the Body of Christ. In the natural order of creation, they claim, men are superior to women. Conservative Christians are especially fond of arguing that in Christ there is neither male nor female, but among men, women are inferior. Ironically, many of these same people maintain that within the "spiritual" church the "natural" order of inequality should rule. Others work within the same

straitjacket, but conclude that Paul contradicts himself by holding both
to Gnostic equality and female subordination.

From our elaboration of the biblical teachings we would expect that
Paul would affirm neither a Gnostic equalizing of the sexes nor male
supremacy, but that he would stress the partnership of man and woman
in fulfilling the one office of mankind. With this idea in mind, we will
examine certain controversial passages in 1 Corinthians 11 and 14 as well
as 1 Timothy 2, dealing with the place of the woman in worship services,
and Colossians 3:18–19 and Ephesians 5:22–23 which talk of marriage.

Women in Paul's Day

Paul's statements become clearer when we know something about the
place of women in Paul's day. Christian women were just beginning to
realize their freedom in Christ after generations of being denied even
basic rights in the existing cultures. Some of them, no doubt, were
hampered by the general ignorance common to the members of an
inferior social class. Some who were not prepared for their new freedom
may have responded to the Gnostics who denied all sexual differences.
These women started to behave in ways unbecoming to the gospel of
Jesus Christ. They dominated discussions whether or not they had
anything to contribute; they took pride in disagreeing with their husbands in public gatherings; at times they apparently left their husbands
much as the men had issued them writs of divorce on a whim. They
missed Paul's point altogether in that in Christ they were liberated to
be fellow workers alongside men. Instead they were bent on turning the
tables on the men, usurping their place, and seizing all the authority for
themselves.

Paul called women back to order. He reminded them that God is a
God of order and they ought to behave so that the cause of Christ might
be furthered rather than scandalized. Thus, in the culture of that time
Paul demanded that women should wear veils, wear their hair long (1

Cor. 11), keep quiet during discussions in worship services (1 Cor. 14), and refrain from teaching (1 Tim. 2). Paul was not out to suppress women. In fact, his letters suggest that he was deeply moved by their general ignorance and immaturity. Other times he praises God for their service in the church, naming eight women (seven if Junia is masculine) among the twenty-six church leaders in Romans 16. He calls Phoebe deacon (*diakonos*, Rom. 16:1). Prisca (Priscilla) and her husband, Aquila, were Paul's "fellow workers in Christ Jesus" (Rom. 16:3). Paul also names Apphia, Euodia, and Syntyche as church leaders (Philem. 2 and Phil. 4:2 ff.).

"Headship" in 1 Corinthians 11

In 1 Corinthians 11, we find Paul telling women to wear veils because "the head of every man is Christ; and the head of the woman is the man; and the head of Christ is God" (v. 3, KJV). If we conclude from this passage that man is by nature (ontically) superior to woman, we must likewise conclude that Christ is subordinate by nature to God. The church has denied the second conclusion; it is time she emphatically rejects the first.

Paul's meaning rests on the word *head*. Whatever the full meaning of *headship* in 1 Corinthians, it is apparent that an important aspect of the concept is "prominence," especially in reference to being determinative because of its relation of origin.[3] *Head* does not mean "lord," but is virtually synonymous with "beginning" or "origin." This reading makes excellent sense in all of its New Testament occurrences. The focus is on the derivation of woman from man. The passage in 1 Corinthians says in negative terms:

Without Christ from out of whom and in relation to whom man exists, there is no man,

Without man from out of whom and in relation to whom woman exists, there is no woman,

137

Without God from out of whom and in relation to whom Christ exists, there is no Christ.

This passage says the same thing as the Genesis passage about the place and nature of woman: she has no existence in herself, but then neither has man. She can only be defined in relation to man. Later Paul declares that neither can man be fully man without woman and both can only be defined in relation to Christ and through Christ to God. Paul is defending the male-female distinction, without claiming that women are inferior.

Having made his point, Paul adds that failing to wear veils during prophesy and prayer signified a woman's refusal to act as a woman and involved rebellion against God and man. To appear without a veil in Paul's time was unwomanly and shameful. At the same time, non-Christian Corinthian women apparently removed their veils during religious observances. Therefore Paul also wants to distinguish the conduct of Christian women from that of pagan worshipers. He notes ironically that if women do not wear veils, they might as well shave off their hair (reputedly the custom of prostitutes of the time). Today, neither a veil nor the length of a woman's hair suggests that she accepts or rejects her role as a woman. Neither one distinguishes Christian from non-Christian conduct. Instead modern life demands that we guard against blurring the sexual distinction and that we develop a distinctive Christian life-style in other ways.

Woman: Glory of Man

In verses 7 and following of 1 Corinthians 11 Paul expands his argument by asserting that a woman ought to cover her head and a man ought not to cover his head because man "is the image and glory of God: but the woman is the glory of the man. For the man is not of the woman; but the woman of the man. Neither was the man created for the woman; but the woman for the man. For this cause ought the woman to have power on her head because of the angels" (KJV).

But it is wrong to stop at this point. Paul still has more to say. He rephrases the argument to avoid possible misunderstandings. "Nevertheless," he continues, "neither is the man without the woman, neither the woman without the man, in the Lord. For as the woman is of the man, even so is the man also by the woman; but all things of God" (1 Cor. 11:11–12, KJV).

A careful reading of the entire passage indicates that Paul is not championing the superiority of man over woman but stressing their biunity, mutuality, and reciprocity in their difference. The phrase "the woman for the man" (v. 9) does not mean that woman was made to serve man. In terms of Genesis 2:18, it underlines God's intention that woman was made to be a helper and partner for man.

Although the full meaning of *glory* is not yet clear, it certainly carries the connotation of the Hebrew word for glory *(kabod)* which means "weight."[4] When a man has "weight," he has "worth," "importance," "honor"—glory. To describe a person as the glory of someone else is to define that person in terms of the one he reveals.

When man is the man of God, he has "weight" and "importance"; he is the glory of God. He is a living demonstration or image of his Maker, and he knows that weight is of the Lord. Man, as the glory of God, reflects and images God. In a similar way when a woman has "weight" and "importance," she is really woman and the glory of man. She is the glory of man because only with him can she really be woman and because only with her can he be fully man. Only when women and men both realize that their existence is impossible without each other can mankind (male and female) really show to best advantage.

Another difficult portion of 1 Corinthians 11 is the sentence, "For this cause ought the woman to have power on her head because of the angels" (KJV). The "power" or "authority" *(exousia)* that a woman is to have on her head is commonly thought to be a sign of the power of the men to which women must be subjected. However, this interpretation has no philological support; in no other Scripture passage does *exousia* mean powerlessness, as this interpretation suggests. Furthermore, the context of the verse offers no support for this view. It makes bétter sense to think of *exousia* as a sign of woman's own authority.[5] A veil is a sign that man does not know his calling; for a woman it is a sign that she knows her calling. Not to wear a veil would mean she refused to accept her calling, yielding to sinful pride over against God. The phrase, "because of the angels," emphasizes that God is indeed present because angels represent God's presence in worship services.

Silence in the Churches

In 1 Corinthians 14 Paul argues that woman "are not permitted to speak, but should be subordinate, as even the law says" (v. 34). Often commentators assume that "subordinate" means "subordinate to man." But that is an unfounded assumption. The text simply does not say that. In the same way it is presumptuous to claim, as many do, that Paul's reference to the law means Genesis 3:16.[6] Would Paul be appealing to the curse as the Law? Is it not reasonable to assume that he has special reference to the creation story as he does in 1 Timothy 2? Women are to help men as copartners. When we take Paul's words in their full context, they come down to something like this: "Women, you are not above the law; you too are under obedience as the law directs, but since you are abdicating your lawful office of co-worker with man, you should keep quiet."

The context strongly supports this interpretation. In 1 Corinthians 14:35 Paul further admonishes women to ask their husbands at home if they have questions. Since Paul connects the silence of women with their desire to learn, he seems to be warning women that they were speaking out of ignorance. His prohibition, then, is against their unprofitable interruptions in the assemblies. His stringent measures must also be understood against the background of the fact that the teaching of women in the synagogues was completely foreign to Jewish law.[7] If changes are to be made in this sensitive area—and Paul favors them—

they must be for the better. Paul is not forbidding all participation of women in worship services, but he is forbidding women to speak in the part of the service involving dialogue-type discussion. Then the women were apparently at their bickering best, trying to embarrass, if not defy, their husbands. To stop such unedifying and confusing spectacles (" . . . so that the church may be edified. For God is not a God of confusion but of peace," 1 Cor. 14:5, 33), Paul issues his edict calling women to task. He is not deriding them, but urging them to obey their calling as women.

The usual interpretation is that Paul is here forbidding all feminine participation in worship services. However, those who take this view face the real problem that Paul allows women to prophesy and pray in 1 Corinthians 11. Some try to avoid the contradiction involved by saying that 1 Corinthians 11 is not talking about prophesy and prayer in official worship services.[8] Since there is no evidence for this at all, Paul must either be contradicting himself (which I find unacceptable) or his prohibition is more limited than is usually thought.

Significantly many regard Paul's call to women to be silent in the church as universal norm, whereas they do not do this with Paul's plea for veils even though it occurs in the same context and is justified by the same general norm. To select one call as relevant for today but not the other is simply arbitrary. Many point out that the last part of 1 Corinthians 14:33, "as in all the churches of the saints" actually belongs to verse 34: "the women should keep silence in the churches." However, it is both logical and grammatically acceptable to leave the phrase with the earlier part of verse 33. "For God is not a God of confusion but of peace, as in all the churches of the saints." Paul sets forth a universal norm that holds for all time. Then, to expedite the general norm of peace and order Paul disallows the speaking of women in the Corinthian church.

Even if the phrase is read with verse 34, why must we conclude that Paul had in mind all churches throughout history? Throughout Corinthians Paul emphasizes that unity of the church is so important that no contradictory customs and arrangements should spring up in the community (cf. 1 Cor. 4:17; 7:17; 11:16). Of course, that is excellent advice, but does Paul mean that every church in history must have the same customs, including silence for women? The answer, I believe, is no. Customs may differ from time to time. The important matter is that these customs, whatever they are, specify and particularize universal biblical norms. Today we need to take the basic norms given in Scripture and concretize them for our situation. Only in this way can we avoid the subjectivism and arbitrariness involving in picking and choosing which specific stipulations are normative and which are not.

Woman As Man's Partner

In many ways 1 Timothy 2:8–15 intensifies 1 Corinthians 14. "Let the woman learn in silence with all subjection. But I suffer not a woman to teach, nor to usurp authority over the man, but to be in silence" (1 Tim. 2:11–12, kjv). Paul is upset by the disturbing antics of women in the congregation. In a construction corresponding to that of 1 Corinthians 14, he commands them to be silent and to learn in subjection. Again, it is important to note that the text does not read "subjection to men." Women are to be subject to the demands of the law of God for women. Moreover, Paul forbade women to teach in the same breath that he told them not to domineer men. Apparently this is another situation like the one in Corinth: women were apparently interrupting the services to embarrass and perhaps domineer the men.

It is worth noting that Paul does not say women cannot exercise authority over men.[9] Rather women are not to domineer men and dictate *(authentien)* to them. In so doing, women break their partnership relation with men and usurp God's authority over men as well as women.

In this context Paul's reasons for insisting that women learn in silence and refrain from teaching take on added meaning. He writes, "For Adam was formed first, then Eve; and Adam was not deceived, but the woman" (1 Tim. 2:13, 14). If we keep the previous discussion in mind, the main lines of Paul's argument become clear. Paul is not saying that women are to be in subjection to *man* because Adam was first formed, as many assume. Rather, Paul insists that women learn they are to be helpmates for men—in that way, being subject to God's will for women —and not competitors aiming to dominate; for Adam was created first, then Eve to be a partner for man. Moreover, it was not Adam who was first deceived but Eve. Paul is not denying that Adam sinned (cf. Rom. 5:12), but he is emphasizing Eve's deception. Mankind's trouble began when Eve set aside her partnership role with man under God. She was deceived and then proceeded to dominate man and lead him astray.

Again, as in 1 Corinthians 14, Paul apparently realizes that his strong language could lead readers to think that he has no use for women at all. "Yet," he adds, "women will be saved through bearing children, if she continues in faith and love and holiness, with modesty" (1 Tim. 2:15). Paul is clearly alluding to Genesis 3:16, but he is also taking a gibe at the Gnostics, who rejected marriage (cf. 1 Tim. 4:3). He exclaims that a woman will be saved as a woman—if she continues in faith. In Genesis, woman in her totality was cursed in terms of one of her typical tasks. In the same way, Paul proclaims that woman can be saved in her totality in terms of the same typical task—if she continues in obedience in all she does.

Subjection in Marriage

We have yet to deal with Paul's passages on marriage, Colossians 3:18 and 19, Ephesians 5:22–23, and 1 Peter 3:1. Since all three passages speak of women being in subjection to their husbands, it is important to notice the significant role that the concept of subjection or submissiveness plays in the whole New Testament. Nowhere does subjection mean inferiority. Christ was subject unto his parents (Luke 2:51). Christ himself will subject himself to the Father (1 Cor. 15:28). The subjection in these passages has to do with obeying one's calling, being subject to the demands of the office. No where does it say that women are to be subject to men. However, in the office of wife, a woman is to subject herself to her husband.

Ephesians 5:21 ("Submitting yourselves one to another in the fear of God," KJV) emphasizes that members of Christ's body must submit themselves to one another in the fear of the Lord in order to fulfill their calling. Peter also exhorts the people to submit to the elders and to one another, even as he exhorts elders not to lord it over the flock (1 Pet. 5:5). Paul's call to submission is particularly important because in the next verse he specifies, telling wives to be subject to their own husbands. Submitting to one another does not involve in the least the idea of being substandard; rather it is the calling to serve each other in order to fulfill God's demands.

Thus Paul never implies that women are deficient or inferior even when he reminds wives to be subject to their husbands in such passages as Ephesians 5:22 ("Wives, be subject to your husbands, as to the Lord") and Colossians 3:18 ("Wives, be subject to your husbands, as is fitting in the Lord"). More than that, the focus is not so much on the wives and husbands as it is on the offices of wife and husband in relation to each other, not so much on the individuals involved as on the norm for marriage. In effect, Paul says, "Be wives as is fitting in the Lord, that is, as the norm for marriage instructs. Submit to your husbands as wives in the Lord, that is, as the Word of God for marriage requires."

The mutuality of marriage relations is especially striking when we see that in Ephesians 5:25 Paul immediately adds, "Husbands, love your wives, as Christ loved the church and gave himself up for her" and in Colossians 3:19, "Husbands, love your wives, and do not be harsh with them." Even as he instructs wives to be good wives, he exhorts husbands to be good husbands. In fact Paul spends nine verses exhorting husbands to love their wives, while he directs four verses to wives. Apparently the husbands were often as guilty as the wives. Remember, says Paul, what Christ did for the church. The care that he shows is something for you to take to heart in your marriages. In Colossians Paul bluntly tells the husbands not to be harsh to their wives. Apparently the wives have some legitimate grievances, but the solution is neither running away nor a writ of divorce. Instead, it is living up to the calling of being wife and husband.

To conclude from these texts that women do not have to love their husbands is as preposterous as to claim that husbands do not have to submit to their wives. Paul is calling both husbands and wives to obedience to the norm of marriage. This involves mutual love and mutual submission. The mutuality is heightened even more when we recall that in Christ's life "submission" and "love" were synonymous. To love is to serve. Christ emphasized the service concept of office in direct contrast to any of the other concepts in existence at that time. Six times in the synoptic gospels we read that the greatest must be the servant of all (Matt. 20:26–28, 23:11; Mark 9:35, 10:43–45; Luke 9:48, 22:26–27). Naturally, then, Christ requires that husband and wife submit to each other in love and thus obey the will of God.

1 Peter 3:1 deserves mention because, in an indirect way, it confirms our contention that being in subjection does not mean being bossed around. Wives are to be in subjection to their husbands so that, if any be unbelievers, they may perhaps be won for Christ by the behavior of their wives. Obviously, subjection does not entail authority to forbid wives from believing in Christ. Like Paul, Peter is calling wives and husbands to their offices. Wives are not to be show-offs and play the role of loose women. Likewise, husbands are to act with understanding and to honor the wife as the weaker[10] because they are equally heirs of the grace of life (1 Pet. 3:7).

For a moment we should return to Ephesians 5:23 where Paul gives the reason that wives are to be subject to their husbands. "For the husband is the head of the wife as Christ is the head of the church, his body, and is himself its Savior." As in our previous discussion of headship, Paul cannot be proclaiming the husband's superiority. He is saying that the husband has a special role in marriage and that it is necessary for the wife to recognize it or she cannot be a wife. This does not mean to say that the husband should always rule. No. Paul is again stressing the mutuality of the roles. Recognizing their places as wife and husband, the partners must do everything in accordance with the norm of troth. Thus, continues Paul, even as the church is subject to Christ and recognizes that she is church and not her own savior, so a wife is not to forget her role of wife, but is to be subject; that is, she is to be a wife to her husband in everything. The meaning of the husband's headship is further articulated in the section on marriage. Concerning Paul's teaching on the mutuality of marriage, we should recall 1 Corinthians 7:3, 4: "The husband should give to his wife her conjugal rights, and likewise the wife to her husband. For the wife does not rule over her own body, but the husband does, likewise the husband does not rule over his own body, but the wife does."

Clearly, our usual Judaistic-Hellenistic idea of subordination does not fit the Pauline texts on the place of women. Only the creation-idea of partnership set forth in Genesis does justice to these Scripture passages.

NOTES

1. For a detailed discussion of Paul's ideas on women and a summary of the previous literature on the subject, see Else Kähler's *Die Frau in den Paulinischen Briefen Unter Besonderer Berücksichtigung des Begriffes der Unterordnung* (Zurich: Gotthelf-Verlag, 1960). Krister Stendahl's *The Bible and The Role of Women* (Philadelphia: Fortress Press, 1966) also deserves notice. For the special situation in Corinth, W. Schmithal's *Gnosticism in Corinth* (Nashville: Abingdon Press, 1971) is valuable. After this appendix was written my attention was called to Dick and Joyce Boldrey's "Women in Paul's Life," *Trinity Studies*, 2 (1972), pp. 1–36. The Boldreys' excellent essay is more detailed and comes to the same conclusion as I do on virtually every point.

2. For example, Georg Gunter Blum's well-documented and detailed article, "The Office of Woman in the New Testament" in *Why Not? Priesthood and*

the Ministry of Women, ed. M. Bruce and G. E. Duffield (Abingdon: Marcham Manor Press, 1972) is severely weakened by this confusion. He writes that "it is more likely that St. Paul starts from the general subordination of women to their husbands, due to the Creation, i.e., the Fall" (p. 69). Indeed, merging creation and Fall, Blum cannot avoid tension between creation and redemption, rather than between Fall and redemption. "The circumstances of Creation have been transformed sacramentally by Redemption, though they are still valid for the concrete ordering of the community" (p. 71). Likewise in their Biblical Commentary on the Old Testament, The Pentateuch, vol. 1 (Grand Rapids: Eerdmans, 1951), p. 103, C. F. Keil and F. Delitzsch confuse the Creation and Fall by explaining the subordination of women to be "divinely appointed" in creation and increased in the Fall so that she had a "desire bordering upon disease." Larry Christenson in The Christian Family also grounds the subordination "upon the creation." "It is further grounded upon the fall" (p. 39). Krister Stendahl in The Bible and the Role of Woman identifies the Law with Gen. 1–3 (p. 30) without regard for the fact that Gen. 3 gives us the dis-order of the Fall. Failing to distinguish the partnership of creation from the subordination of the Fall, he is forced later to write that Gal. 3:28 is both "directed against what we call the order of creation," (that is, subordination), and in tension with passages "by which this order of creation maintains its place in the fundamental view of the N.T. concerning the subordination of women" (p. 32, cf. also 34).

3. See the discussion of head in Theological Dictionary of the New Testament, vol. 3, ed. Gerhard Kittel (Grand Rapids: Eerdmans, 1965), pp. 673–82. Also Herman N. Ridderbos, Paulus (Kampen: Kok, 1966) pp. 420–32 and Clarence Vos, Woman in the Old Testament Worship (Delft: Judels and Brinkman, 1968), pp. 28–31.

4. See the discussion of glory in Theological Dictionary of the New Testament, vol. 2, ed. Gerhard Kittel (Grand Rapids: Eerdmans, 1964), pp. 233–53.

5. In 1 Cor. 8:9 exousia is in fact translated as "liberty" or "freedom." See James Hurley, "Did Paul Require Veils or the Silence of Women? A Consideration of 1 Cor. 11:2–16 and 1 Cor. 14:33b–36," Westminster Theological Journal 36 (1973), pp. 206–12. Also Gerhard Kittel, Rabbinica (1920), pp. 17–31. Hurley also promotes the interesting idea that Paul was not concerned about veils or no-veils, but hair-up or hair-down (pp. 196–204).

6. For example, F. W. Grosheide, Commentary on the First Epistle to the

Corinthians (Grand Rapids: Eerdmans, 1953) p. 343; also see Blum's article, p. 68, cited in note 2.

7. It is possible that *law* in v. 34 refers only to the Jewish law excluding women from prayer.

8. For example, Grosheide, pp. 252, 341–42.

9. The RSV wrongly translates "I permit no woman to have authority over men." The JB reads the same prejudice into the passage, "I am not giving permission for a woman . . . to tell a man what to do." The KJV is much closer to the original "But I suffer not a woman to teach, nor to usurp authority over the man." The New English Bible has "domineer."

10. "Weaker vessel," KJV. The RSV prejudices the matter with "the weaker sex." The wives were weaker socially, politically and underdeveloped intellectually. Physical weakness is not the point. "Vessel" is the same word Paul uses in 1 Thess. 4:4 (KJV), which the RSV translates "wife." Husbands are to honor their wives "in holiness and honor" even if they are culturally considered to be without power.